The First Christians

Keeping the Faith in Times of Trouble

by

Gerard M. Verschuuren

En Route Books and Media, LLC
5705 Rhodes Avenue
St. Louis, MO 63109

Cover credit: TJ Burdick

LCCN: 2018936027

Copyright © 2018 Gerard M. Verschuuren
All rights reserved.

ISBN-13: 978-0-9998814-1-5
ISBN-10: 0-9998814-1-8

TABLE OF CONTENTS

PREFACE 1

1. WHO WERE THE FIRST CHRISTIANS? 3
    a. Their Bible 3
    b. Closer to Jesus, the source of it all 7
    c. Christians or Catholics? 12

2. THE 1ST GENERATION (30-80) 19
    a. Backdrop 19
    b. Trouble Within: Ebionism 27
    c. Defenders of the Faith 32
        Simon Peter (1-67) 32
        Paul of Tarsus (5-67) 39
        Didache (c. 75) 44

3. THE 2ND GENERATION (80-130) 49
    a. Backdrop 49
    b. Trouble Within: Docetism 53
    c. Defenders of the Faith 56
        Clement of Rome (?-99) 56
        Ignatius of Antioch (35-108) 63

4. THE 3RD GENERATION (130-180) 71
    a. Backdrop 71
    b. Trouble Within: Gnosticism 75
    c. Defenders of the Faith 80
        Polycarp of Smyrna (69-155) 80
        Justin Martyr (100-165) 85
        Irenaeus of Lyons (130-202) 93

5. THE 4TH GENERATION (180-230) 105
    a. Backdrop 105
    b. Trouble Within: Montanism 108
    c. Defenders of the Faith 111
        Clement of Alexandria (150-215) 111

    Tertullian of Carthage (160-220) 117

6. THE 5ᵀᴴ GENERATION (230-280) 125

   a. Backdrop *125*
   b. Trouble Within:Adoptionism/Novatianism 128
   c. Defenders of the Faith *130*
      Origen (184-253) *130*
      Cyprian of Carthage (210-258) *135*

7. THE 6ᵀᴴ GENERATION (280-330) 145

   a. Backdrop *145*
   b. Trouble Within:Modalism/Patripassianism 148
   c. Defenders of the Faith *150*
      Lactantius (240-320) *150*
      Alexander of Alexandria (c. 250-327) *156*

8. THE 7ᵀᴴ GENERATION (330-380) 163

   a. Backdrop *163*
   b. Trouble Within: Arianism *165*
   c. Defenders of the Faith *175*
      Athanasius of Alexandria (295-373) *175*
      Basil of Caesarea (330-379) *181*
      Gregory of Nazianzus (330-390) *186*
      Gregory of Nyssa (335-394) *191*
      Hilary of Poitiers (300-368) *195*

9. THE 8ᵀᴴ GENERATION (380-430) 205

   a. Backdrop *205*
   b. Trouble Within: Donatism | Pelagianism.. *209*
   c. Defenders of the Faith *213*
      Jerome (347-420) *213*
      Augustine of Hippo (354-440) *219*

10. THE 9ᵀᴴ GENERATION (430-480) 231

   a. Backdrop *231*
   b. Trouble Within: Nestorianism *235*
   c. Defenders of the Faith *237*
      Cyril of Alexandria (378-444) *237*
      John Cassian (c. 360-c. 435) *243*

11.	CONCLUSION	251
12.	FOR FURTHER READING	257
13.	INDEX	259
ABOUT THE AUTHOR		259

Preface

The First Christians, who are the subject of this book, span a period of some five hundred years. That may seem a long time to still call them "the *first* Christians," but the word "first" is a rather broad notion—as broad as the term "the *early* Christians" would be. It does not mean "the very first Christians"—for that would be the apostles or so—but rather the Christians of the five first centuries AD.

A period of five hundred years may seem long, but it is relatively short given the extensive history of Christianity, stretching over two millennia. Think of the first Native Americans; they had lived in the Americas some ten million years before the Spanish conquistadores invaded the continent. But they were still its "first" inhabitants. Time is just a relative and flexible notion. The same holds for the expression "the first Christians." Compared to us, they were "first" before we ourselves came along, and they were "first" to experience Jesus after he had come to live among us. They were nearest to the apostles, who were, in turn, nearest to Jesus.

In this book, we speak about these first Christians mainly through the people who gave them a voice and a compass: the Church Fathers. They were their leaders and their teachers, heirs to the apostles. They were also the ones to tell us present-day Christians about the deep Faith of the first

Christians. They told us how these Christians could keep the Faith in times of trouble—even in very tumultuous times, when they were constantly besieged from two sides: by prosecution from without and by heresies from within. The Church Fathers kept their flock together and kept them on the right path. We can only understand the Church Fathers if we understand them as *fathers* who deeply cared about the newborn Church as if it were their own family. They are Fathers with a "pedigree."

I tried to let the Church Fathers speak for themselves, as much as possible. To do so I used a translation of their words that is easily accessible on the Internet, so you can check its accuracy and the context in which these words were spoken and written. This translation may not always be smooth, and the way the Church Fathers expressed themselves may not always be clear to modern ears, but their words deserve serious attention, for they are the pillars on which the Church has built what Catholics believe—now and then. They are a vital part of our history and tradition, dating back to Jesus Christ himself.

I decided to focus on what the Church Fathers did for us to keep our Faith authentic and uncorrupted, without any deviations from the original message we were given by the first generation of Christians who had lived with Jesus himself and had seen and heard Jesus with their own eyes and ears. But once Jesus had gone back to the Father, we would depend on others to tell us about what Jesus had told us. That's where the Church Fathers come in.

1. Who Were the First Christians?

Most Christians have some kind of fascination with the early Church: that's where it all began, with the first enthusiasm and the first intensity. After that, things seem to have winded down. Some even say it went dramatically downhill.

Fascination with the beginnings of something is rather common. We love to go back to what we consider the "romantic" origin of whatever that "something" is—whether it is about science and its first scientists, or space exploration and its first astronauts, or the US Constitution and its Founding Fathers. We love to adorn all "founding fathers" with a halo. Think of Galileo among the first scientists, or John Glenn among the first astronauts, or Samuel Adams among the first framers of the American Constitution. Why should we not do the same for the First Christians?

a. Their Bible

Especially since the Protestant Reformation, many Christians believe that the first Christians were rooted in the Bible and emerged from the Bible, more in particular the New Testament. They think the apostles carried the New Testament with them and distributed copies of it among their new followers. That is indeed a very romantic view. However, the reverse of this is actually true: the New Testament did not start the Early Church but was a product of the Early Church. The first Christians did not have a Bible yet. Of course, they had the Hebrew Scriptures—which they typically referred to when they spoke of "the Scriptures," and which we now call the Old Testament—but their New Testament was still in the making, right in the middle of the Early Church. Today, we live in a society in which the written word is more prevalent than the spoken word, but that is a rather recent development. In ancient cultures much was passed on by spoken tradition before it was gradually written down on "paper."

In other words, when the Holy Spirit fell upon the apostles at Pentecost, the purpose was to give birth to the Church, not to deliver a manuscript. It was the Church's task to first develop the New Testament by writing down what Jesus had taught his followers and what they had experienced in living with him. And then the next step was to determine which written down accounts were reliable and which were not. This means that the Early Church had to establish what is called the *canon*—an official list of inspired New Testament books. She had to separate the inspired wheat from the uninspired chaff. In other words, every Bible has a very important page that did not come with all the books we find in the Bible—and that is its table of contents.

How could those earliest Christians have lived by "Scripture alone," when they had only the Hebrew Scriptures, but nothing about Jesus yet? The answer is that they had all that was needed. They knew Jesus either from personal experience or from the experiences of the ones who had been with Jesus. They were direct or indirect witnesses of what Jesus had said and done while being in the flesh. Christianity is not a religion of the Book but a religion of the Word that became flesh.

The First Christians: Keeping the Faith in Times of Trouble

Until the early 5th century, Bible canons were mostly an affair of local churches. What belongs to the Bible, and what does not, had to be *gradually* decided by the Church. She did not receive the Bible ready-made from Christ himself or the apostles; she went by what was being used and read in her liturgy. The oldest surviving list is the *Muratorian Canon*, from around 150. The so-called *Muratorian Fragment* is a copy of perhaps the oldest known list of most of the books of the New Testament. It was discovered around 1740 in the Ambrosian Library in Milan by Father Muratori. The fragment, consisting of 85 lines, was written in barbarous Latin, and was most likely translated from an original written in Greek about 160 (Greek was the language prevailing in Christian Rome until c. 200). It consists of all that remains of a section of a list of all the works that were accepted as canonical by the churches known to its original compiler. The unidentified author accepts four Gospels, the "Acts of all Apostles," thirteen of Paul's Letters, the Letters of James and Jude, and the Apocalypse of John. The Letter to the Hebrews is not mentioned in the list.

Apparently, it is not exactly the complete canon we use nowadays, for the official canon was still far from settled. Later on, Origen (see 6.c) included the Letter to the Hebrews, but also the Didache (see 2.c) and the Shephard of Hermas. Cyprian of Carthage, on the other hand, rejected Hebrews, James, and Jude. The earliest list that matches exactly the 27 books of the New Testament as we know the canon today comes from Athanasius of Alexandria (see 8.c). He promulgated that list in the year 367, and said it was binding on the whole Church. But there remained disputes. If it is not the Bible that determines the correct canon, then it must be the Church. For if it were not the Church who determines the correct canon, then we could easily end up with multiple denominations, which keep splitting into smaller and smaller sects, each creating their own Bible canon, leading to a very fragmented Christianity. In other words, it is not up to each individual Christian to determine which books are canonical and orthodox, and therefore should be included in Scripture. The Bible is a book that came from the very heart of the Church; as a matter of fact, the Church authorized the New Testament. So it is the Church who "owns" Scripture—individuals do not.

And this is indeed what happened. The Tradition of the Church decided to omit a few Gospels—for instance, the Gospel of Peter plus all the gospels of "gnostic" origin (see 4.b)—because they went against her tradition and were not used in her liturgies. Soon more detailed common guidelines were developed. It was not until the Synod of Rome in 382, under Pope Damasus I, and the Councils of Hippo in 393 and Carthage in 397 that we find a definitive list of canonical books having been drawn up, and each of these Councils acknowledged the very same list of books. It was ultimately the early Church—not the Bible itself, of course—who determined which books should be included in the Bible.

Many Protestants still think that the history of the Church ended with the closure of the New Testament and picked up again with the sixteenth century Protestant Reformation. In this view, all we need to know about the early Church can be found in the New Testament, more in particular the Acts of the Apostles. But the apostles taught the early Christians much more than the Bible tells us; they told them also about the structure, the praxis, and the liturgy of the early Church—and, most importantly, how we should read and interpret the Scriptures. So this raises the question: where else can we find what the first Christians believed? The answer is in the early Church Fathers who had known the apostles directly or indirectly, were taught by the apostles, and handed down what they had learned from the apostles.

b. Closer to Jesus, the source of it all

Christianity is a religion unique among all religions. Because it is a religion of the "Word made Flesh," all attention and focus is on Jesus: who sees him sees God. So the closer we can get to Jesus, the closer we get to God. Jesus is the focal point of Christianity and its point of origin. We can't get closer to Jesus—in time, that is—than looking at the first generation of Christianity, of those who had lived with Jesus, had seen him act, and had heard him speak. As he had said to his apostles, when calling them: "Come and see." We ourselves can't physically come and see anymore, but we can look at and listen to those who were physically and spiritually close to him. This calls for a way "back to the sources."

"Back to the sources" has been used in various contexts such as the Renaissance and the Reformation, but more recently also in the Second Vatican Council, where it became known as "ressourcement"—literally, back to the sources. This doesn't mean that what happened after the Church Fathers is no longer relevant, but it makes the Church Fathers a vital link between what happened after them and the source of it all, Jesus. Many perhaps thought we were getting back to the time when the Church was still young and not yet corrupted. But the surprise discovery of ressourcement was that the young Church was surprisingly similar to the Church we know nowadays.

That is certainly surprising, for we tend to think that the further we get away from Jesus, the more tainted his original message becomes. When time progresses, the original enthusiasm of the first Christians tends to become diluted, so it seems. Therefore, we want to go back to the time when the Church was still young—young, and not yet corrupted. One of the reasons why we think that the early Church was more genuine and pure than today is that she had not been contaminated yet by devious developments that pulled her away from her origin. It is rather common to think that the further we get away from Jesus—in time, that is—the more chance there is that the original purity gets tainted and corrupted by later developments.

True, over time, the Church may be exposed not only to waning enthusiasm but also to disruptions from within—heresies and schisms. So, being further away from Jesus also means more exposure to deviations: schisms and heresies. Church Father Irenaeus, for instance, saw very clearly that each new generation is exposed to new opportunities for Satan and his heretics (see 4.c). So this poses the question: what is wrong with heresies and schisms?

Let's start with heresies. The word *heresy* comes from the Greek word for "choice." It leads to selective picking and choosing—for instance, only one covenant, only one Gospel, only one apostle, and so on. It chooses a half or incomplete truth over the whole truth. Especially nowadays, many tend to see heresy in terms of a violation of "freedom of expression." In this assessment, there are no heretical views—they are merely harmless, perhaps dissident, alternative views. However, no one would defend such a position if it were about science, for instance: saying that disinfection before surgery makes no sense is not just an alternative view but is definitely "anathema" in science. Something similar holds for heresy in Christianity—it is anathema.[1] Sometimes a heresy is an untruth, but often it is

---

[1] In the New Testament, *anathema* was initially used by the

a faulty, partial truth—not a total lie but a firmly held half-truth that needs to be contested, corrected, and supplemented.

In the New Testament, the apostles were deeply imbued with the conviction that they must transmit the deposit of the Faith to posterity undefiled, and that any teaching at variance with their own—a heresy—would be a culpable offense that should warrant exclusion from the communion of the Church. From very early on, the New Testament tells us how the Christian community was forced to confront those people who persisted in teachings contrary to the Apostolic Faith. The Apostle Paul, for instance, is very adamant that heresies do and will arise within the Church. In the Acts of the Apostles, he says, "I know that after my departure fierce wolves will come in among you, not sparing the flock; and from among your own selves will arise men speaking perverse things, to draw away the disciples after them."[2] Clearly, heresies are a perpetual threat to the Faith.

And what about schisms? In schisms, one separates from the Catholic Church, possibly without heretically repudiating a defined doctrine. Schisms are a threat to the unity of the Church—they split the Christian community into factions and sects. Usually, but not necessarily, the incentive behind a schism is a heresy. The Apostle Paul is very aware of the danger that schisms pose. He warns the Corinthian Church about rivalries among them: "I mean that each of you is saying, 'I belong to Paul,' or 'I belong to Apollos,' or 'I belong to Cephas,' or 'I belong to Christ.' Is Christ divided? Was Paul crucified for you? Or were you baptized in the name of

---

Apostle Paul to mean the excommunication of a heretic or an unrepentant heretic that had been excommunicated.

[2] Acts 20: 29-30.

Paul?"³ And in the First Letter of John, it is stated that schisms always start within the Christian family: "They went out from us, but they were not of us; for if they had been of us, they would have continued with us; but they went out, that it might be plain that they are not of us."⁴ The Gospel of Mark could not have made it more clearly that a house divided against itself cannot stand.⁵

The Church Fathers were very aware of the problems schisms and heresies cause to the Church. The common goal of all Church Fathers was to preserve the unity of Christians—the unity in the Person of Jesus Christ and in his message—regardless of the time that is separating them from Jesus. They justified their orthodox doctrine by showing a "chain" [*catena*] of unbroken teaching stretching from Father to Father, back to the apostles, and ultimately to Jesus.

It is this "unbroken chain" of the Church Fathers that connects us directly with Jesus. In this book, we cover most of the Church Fathers until 480, and we divide them into some nine "generations." Of course, this is a rather artificial classification, but it has some advantages that you will hopefully discover while reading this book. Usually a "generation" covers 30 years, but that is more fit for family trees. In this book, we take a generation to span 50 years, because the Church Fathers need at least 20 years to grow up before they take a position in the Church, and before they can hand over the torch to the next generation of Church Fathers. During this process, they passed on and clarified the teaching of the apostles from the 2nd to at least the 5th

---

³ 1 Cor 1:10-13.
⁴ 1 Jo. 2:19.
⁵ Mark 3:25.

century. This way, they helped bring Christianity out of its cradle into adulthood.

They did so by actually using heresies and schisms for a positive purpose. Heresies and schisms forced the Church and her teachers to be ever clearer in their expression of faith, so as to avoid misunderstandings. In order to do so, the early Fathers had to find an appropriate vocabulary and procedure. One of their tools was invoking philosophy to explain more clearly and rigorously what the Christian Faith is about. Philosophy can be an asset—a tool to analyze seeming contradictions in Christian faith—but unfortunately it can also become a hindrance—philosophy run amok. The Fathers tried to follow a healthy middle course.

We will find out in this book that the Church Fathers did not cause a break with the early Church, as some Protestants believe, but actually preserved its original enthusiasm and message. We will learn that, thanks to the Early Fathers, the Church has always stayed close to Jesus in the course of the centuries. Thanks to them, we know much more about the early stages of the Church than many people think or want to believe. Those skeptics can't believe that finding out what the early Church was like might be as simple as opening up the invaluable records about the early days of the Church that the Church Fathers have left behind. They have all the authority—not, indeed, of Scripture—but of history. There is no period of "silence" in Church history. Those who think differently still try to hold on to what Rod Bennett calls the erroneous "gap theory," as if nothing important had happened during this period of time. The Church Fathers kept the torch burning and passed it on from generation to generation. The importance of their role is no longer the "best-kept" secret that some want it to be. Let the Early Church speak for herself!

Even the Protestant Reformer John Calvin had to declare that for the first six centuries of her existence on earth the Church had remained "pure and undefiled." Stephen Ray, a former Baptist Bible teacher who converted to Catholicism, repeatedly tells us that the more he read about the Church Fathers, the more he realized that the Early Church was Catholic and did not support his Evangelical conclusions.

True, the writings of the early Church Fathers were not included in the New Testament, but that does not mean they had no authority. Their texts were highly esteemed, were copied over and over again, and were widely distributed. These writers may not always have expressed their teachings as clearly as they would be expressed in later ages, but they were the seeds from which later developments emerged. When we call the Early Church young, that does not mean that now the Church is old. Perhaps she is older and more mature, but certainly not old. So what is in-between and separates us from the Early Church is not just a period of darkness. It is a period that is very alive, as we will see soon.

c. Christians or Catholics?

Were the members of the early Church "Christians" or were they "Catholics"? Were the Church Fathers "Christians" or were they "Catholics"? It looks like a harmless or trivial question, but it is actually a rather contentious issue.

Both terms have a very early origin. Paul started his missionary travels from the Church of Antioch in Syria, where the name "Christians" was coined: "believers in Christ." As the Acts of the Apostles tells us, "it was in Antioch that the disciples were first called *Christians*."[6] But the term "Catholic" has also a very old origin. The term was first used

---

[6] Acts 11:26.

already during the 1st century, as far as we know, by Ignatius of Antioch: "Wherever the bishop shall appear, there let the multitude [of the people] also be; even as, wherever Jesus Christ is, there is the *Catholic* Church."[7] Given the casual way Ignatius uses the term "catholic," without any further explanation, tells us he expects his readers to know it already as an accepted term. For Ignatius, "Catholic" means that the Church is more than a collection of isolated and disconnected congregations. It is not a regional cult but intended to include all people of the entire world—universal, that is.

What does this mean for us? If you are a Catholic, should you call yourself "Christian," or "Catholic," or even "Roman Catholic"? Or does it not matter whatever label you choose? There is some reason for choosing the term "Catholic," for in many people's minds, to be a Christian is often taken to be a Protestant. One could even make the case that certain Protestant groups have hijacked the term "Christian" as a tag exclusively for them. This is especially true in the Deep South of the USA, where you can hear people say, after they have left the Catholic Church, that they are no longer Catholic but Christian. But even on TV, when you see a "Christian" broadcast, it is usually on a Protestant channel. The pernicious idea behind this is that Catholics are not Christians but devotees of a cult similar to Jehovah's Witnesses or Mormons.

So should we call ourselves "Catholic" then? Why not, for the term "catholic" simply means "universal." The Greek adjective *katholikos* is a contraction of *kata* and *holos*, which means "about the whole" or "universal." When employing the term at the time of early Christianity, Ignatius of Antioch

---

[7] Letter to the Smyrnaeans 8.

and Polycarp of Smyrna were referring to the Church that was already "everywhere," as distinguished from whatever sects, schisms, or splinter groups might have popped up here and there, in opposition to the Catholic Church. So it is actually a very appropriate term, as long as that doesn't mean that Catholics are not "Christian" in the sense of followers of Christ. In fact, they are both—both "Christian" and "Catholic."

So ultimately, both terms are almost equivalent. But terms can change meaning easily. Because there is nowadays a widespread confusion about what "Catholic" and "Christian" ultimately stand for, some have opted for the label "*Roman* Catholic," and in line with that, "the *Roman* Catholic Church." This does indeed remove any uncertainty by making clear whom or what you are specifically referring too, but it is very doubtful that it is a proper term for Catholics and their Church.

Here is why it's a questionable move. Kenneth D. Whitehead explains how the term "Roman Catholic" came in use.[8] That term caught on mostly in English-speaking countries; it was promoted mostly by Anglicans, supporters of the "branch theory" of the Church, namely, that the one, holy, catholic and apostolic Church of the Creed was supposed to consist of three major branches, the Anglican, the Orthodox and the so-called Roman Catholic branch. Something similar happened in predominantly Calvinist countries such as the Netherlands.

Catholics should nevertheless beware of using the term, not only because of its dubious origins in Anglican and Calvinist circles suggesting that there just might be some other

---

[8] In the May/June 2016 issue of "The Catholic Answer."

The First Christians: Keeping the Faith in Times of Trouble

Catholic Church around somewhere besides the Roman one, but also because it often still is used today to suggest that the "Roman Catholic Church" is something other and lesser than the Catholic Church mentioned in the Nicene Creed.

As cited in the Acts of the Apostles, it is true that the followers of Christ early became known as "Christians," for "it was in Antioch that the disciples were first called Christians.[9] Yet, the name "Christian" was never commonly applied to the Church herself. In the New Testament, the Church is simply called "the Church." There was only one! In that early time there were not yet any break-away bodies substantial enough to be rival claimants of the name and from which the Church might ever have to distinguish herself. And the Church Fathers would also just speak of "the Church." But especially since the Protestant Reformation there have been serious break-away groups, which forced some Christians to speak of "the *Roman* Catholic Church," to distinguish her from other Christian churches.

Yet, the Catholic Church never speaks of herself as "the Roman Catholic Church." Nowhere in the 16 documents of the Second Vatican Council, for instance, will you find the term "Roman Catholic." Pope Paul VI signed all the documents of the Second Vatican Council as "I, Paul. Bishop of the Catholic Church." Simply that—"Catholic Church." No mention of "Roman" here! There are references to the Roman curia, the Roman missal, the Roman rite, etc., but when the adjective Roman is applied to the Church herself, it refers to the Diocese of Rome!

So when we talk in the title of this book about "the first Christians," we could as well have said "the first Catholics"

---

[9] Acts 11:26.

instead, although the term itself was not available immediately after Jesus' death. Yet, speaking of "Christians" is fine as long as we don't use it to distinguish them from "Catholics." Especially in the works of the Early Fathers, Catholics are Christians, and Christians are Catholics.

In the 5th century, Vincent of Lérins would define "Catholic" as follows:

> [I]n the Catholic Church itself, all possible care must be taken, that we hold that faith which has been believed everywhere, always, by all. For that is truly and in the strictest sense Catholic, which, as the name itself and the reason of the thing declare, comprehends all universally. This rule we shall observe if we follow universality, antiquity, consent. We shall follow universality if we confess that one faith to be true, which the whole Church throughout the world confesses; antiquity, if we in no wise depart from those interpretations which it is manifest were notoriously held by our holy ancestors and fathers; consent, in like manner, if in antiquity itself we adhere to the consentient definitions and determinations of all, or at the least of almost all priests and doctors.[10]

So what should we do in matters of dissent? Vincent's answer is very clear:

> What then will a Catholic Christian do, if a small portion of the Church have cut itself off from the communion of the universal faith? What, surely, but prefer the soundness of the whole body to the unsoundness of a pestilent and corrupt member? What, if some novel contagion seek to infect not merely an insignificant portion of the Church,

---

[10] Commonitory 6.

> *but the whole? Then it will be his care to cleave to antiquity, which at this day cannot possibly be seduced by any fraud of novelty.*[11]

Vincent realizes this does not answer all our questions. So he keeps probing:

> *But what, if in antiquity itself there be found error on the part of two or three men, or at any rate of a city or even of a province? Then it will be his care by all means, to prefer the decrees, if such there be, of an ancient General Council to the rashness and ignorance of a few. But what, if some error should spring up on which no such decree is found to bear? Then he must collate and consult and interrogate the opinions of the ancients, of those, namely, who, though living in various times and places, yet continuing in the communion and faith of the one Catholic Church, stand forth acknowledged and approved authorities: and whatsoever he shall ascertain to have been held, written, taught, not by one or two of these only, but by all, equally, with one consent, openly, frequently, persistently, that he must understand that he himself also is to believe without any doubt or hesitation.*[12]

In the 4th century, bishop Pacian of Barcelona would say, "Christian is my first name; Catholic is my surname. The former gives me an identity, the latter distinguishes me."[13] How true his statement is. The name "Catholic" does not refer to any heretic like Montanus, Arius, Pelagius, or Donatus. Catholics distinguish themselves from all others—

---

[11] Ibid. 7.
[12] Ibid. 8.
[13] The Extant Works of S. Pacian, Library of Fathers of the Holy Catholic Church 17 (1842) pp. 317-327. Letter 1: On the Catholic Name.

from all Gnostics, Arians, Modalists, or Donatists. Catholics trace their identity back to the "one and only" Jesus Christ.

In other words, all Catholics live in "communion" with each other as belonging to one Catholic Church. This communion, which we call "Church," does not only extend to all Catholic believers in a specific historical period, but also embraces all the epochs and all the generations. Pope Benedict XVI spoke of a "twofold universality": a *synchronic* one (uniting Catholics in every part of the world) as well as a *diachronic* one (uniting all Catholics of the past and of the future).[14] It is the latter one that unites us today with the first Christians through the intermediaries of the Church Fathers. It is this historical link with the First Christians that makes and keeps us Christian and Catholic. It is tradition that unites us with the First Christians. Tradition is the living river that links us to the origins—"back to the sources."

---

[14] General Audience, Wednesday, 26 April 2006.

2. The 1st Generation (30-80)

a. Backdrop

Civil war engulfed the Roman nation in the middle of the 1st century before Christ was born—first between Julius Caesar and Pompey, and finally between Octavian and Mark Antony. Antony was defeated at the Battle of Actium in 31 BC. In 27 BC the Senate and People of Rome made Octavian "commander," thus beginning the first era of Roman imperial history usually dated from 27 BC to AD 284. They later awarded him the name Augustus, "the venerated." Augustus was a member of the Julian family, one of the most ancient patrician clans of Rome, while Tiberius was a member of the Claudia family, only slightly less ancient than the Julians. The so-called Julio-Claudian dynasty lasted for four more emperors—Tiberius, Caligula, Claudius, and Nero—before in AD 69 Vespasian became the founder of the brief Flavian dynasty.

Jesus was born at the time Palestine was part of this large Roman Empire. It was under the Emperor Augustus (27 BC - AD 14) that Jesus was born. It was under the Emperor Tiberius (14-37) that Jesus was crucified. It was under the other three Julio-Claudian emperors that the apostles would spread the Gospel of Jesus through most of the Roman Empire.

Caesar Augustus had been emboldened to declare himself "master of all things." He would eventually transform the democratic Roman Senate into a mere "rubber stamp" committee. This was followed by a rapid succession of emperors, running from Augustus to the powerful Tiberius, to the psychotic Caligula, to the mentally retarded Claudius, and culminating in the perverse Nero—about whom the Church historian Eusebius (c. 324) wrote, "he ran into such blood-guiltiness that he did not spare even his nearest relatives and dearest friends, but destroyed his mother and his brothers and his wife, with very many others of his own family as he would private and public enemies, with various kinds of deaths."[15] It is about this Nero (37-68) that the Roman historian Tacitus wrote that he "inflicted the most exquisite tortures on a class hated for their abominations, called *Christians* by the populace."[16]

Jews had a unique position in the Roman Empire at that time. By the beginning of the first century AD, Jews had spread from their homeland in Judaea across the Mediterranean, and there were major Jewish communities in Syria, Egypt, Greece, and even Rome. Practicing a very different religion from that of their neighbors, they were often unpopular. But they were also somehow protected. Under Julius Caesar, Judaism was officially recognized as a legal religion—a policy followed by the first Roman emperor, Augustus. Herod the Great had been designated "King of the Jews" by the Roman Senate. All of this gave Judaism the status of a "permitted religion" [*religio licita*] throughout the Empire. Synagogues were classified as colleges to get around Roman laws, and Jewish temples were allowed to collect the yearly tax paid by all Jewish men for temple maintenance.

---

[15] History of the Church 2:25.
[16] Annals, book 15, chapter 44.

The First Christians: Keeping the Faith in Times of Trouble

All of this would drastically change in AD 66, when the Jewish population of Judea revolted against Roman rule. In September 70, the Romans took action: the Roman general Titus breached the walls of Jerusalem, sacked the city, and destroyed the Second Temple. And in 73, Roman forces breached the walls of Masada, a mountain fortress held by Jewish extremists. In addition, the separation between Jews and Christians would become more definite when, at the end of the first century, a rupture occurred between the Synagogue and the Church. No longer would Christians be considered a particular group of Jews.

Initially, the Christians did not have their own places of worship—they would meet in the synagogue. But when the "divide" between the Christian "faction" and the Jewish "faction" began to gradually widen, Christians would gather locally in the home of one of the Christians to listen to the Word of God and to celebrate the Eucharist. For instance, in the home of Gaius in Corinth, "who is host to me and to the whole church"[17], or in the home of Nympha in Laodicea, "Give greetings to the brothers in Laodicea and to Nympha and to the church in her house[18], or in the home of Philemon in Colossae, "and to the church at your house."[19] It is exactly this type of locations that they called *ekklesia* in Greek or *ecclesia* in Latin—which means convocation, assembly, or gathering. The homes of Christians would become a "church"—not to be confused with the Church—until true and proper buildings or churches for Christian worship would arise in the 3rd century.

Nevertheless, Christianity was born in the cradle of Judaism.

---

[17] Rom 16:23.
[18] Col. 4:15.
[19] Philem. 1:2.

As Pope Pius IX once said about Christians, "Spiritually we are Semites."[20] At the time Jesus was born, Judaism had been extensively prepared for the coming of the Messiah—*Moshiach* in Hebrew and *Christos* in Greek—and the Jews were eagerly awaiting his arrival. The prophecies of the Old Testament had repeatedly announced his coming. Writings of the Second Temple period, which did not become part of the Old Testament, also spoke of him extensively.[21] And even the Talmud, which contains the teachings and opinions of thousands of rabbis, and also the great Jewish sages of the Middle Ages kept expressing the Messianic hope of Judaism. One of those medieval sages, the legendary Maimonides, who died in AD 1204, considers faith in the coming of the Messiah as one of the "Thirteen Principles" of the Jewish faith.

When some modern Jews deny that a belief in the Messiah is essential to Judaism, they are actually denying a vital part of Jewish history. What their reason is for doing so can only be guessed. Perhaps their claim is mainly motivated by a desire to deter Jews from considering the beliefs of Christianity, for if Jews had never expected a Messiah, they would not have to face any serious questions about Jesus and his Messianic mission.

However, there is undeniable evidence that the Old Testament does express Messianic expectations. It announces in particular that the Messiah is on his way, that he will be descended from David, and that he will bring back Israel—and more in specific, that he will come from Bethlehem, born of a virgin, and that he will do miraculous things, and that he will suffer to atone for our sins. We find

---

[20] Sept. 6, 1938, in a speech to a group of Belgian pilgrims.
[21] between 500 BC and AD 70.

these prophecies all over the Old Testament: in Genesis 49:10, Numbers 24:17, Isaiah 7:14; 6:9-10; 9:1-2; 9:6; 11:1-4; 35:4-7; 53, 61:1-2, 1 Samuel 7:12-13, Micah 5:2, Zechariah 9, 12, 13, Psalm 22, 72, Wisdom 2:12-24, and Daniel 9. It is hard to miss the underlying Messianic message.

True, this Messianic idea becomes more vivid and explicit as one progresses through the Old Testament, in the same way as Moses was given a fuller understanding of God than Abraham, and Abraham received a fuller knowledge than his predecessors. God teaches us progressively, step by step, so we are more and better prepared for what he is about to reveal to us. That's also the way the Jewish people were finally prepared enough for the coming of the Messiah when he did come.

There is some ambiguity, though, in the way the Messiah is described—either as someone who suffers and dies or as someone who comes in power and glory. Interestingly enough, the Talmud has the same ambiguity about what will happen when the Messiah comes. It speaks of two Messiahs: *Messiah ben Joseph* ("Son of Joseph") and *Messiah ben David* ("Son of David"). Christians would rather say that the coming of the Messiah happens twice: he came the first time as a suffering Messiah to redeem us, and he will come a second time in glory to restore us. As a matter of fact, in the New Testament, Jesus is sometimes referred to as "the son of Joseph,"[22] sometimes as "the Son of David."[23] But no matter how we look at it, the Jewish people had been well prepared for his coming—the stage was set for him. Whether they were really ready for his (first) arrival, is another issue, of course.

Apparently, the idea of a Messiah was strong among Jews

---

[22] e.g. Mt. 13:55.
[23] e.g. Mt. 9:27; 21:9.

during the first century. Without the expectation of a Messiah, Jesus could probably have never been accepted as the Messiah. When Jesus asked his apostles, "Who do you say that I am?"[24] Peter—being a Jew and living in the expectation of a Jew—had been prepared to say, "You are the Messiah."

Jesus' question keeps resounding through the history of the Church, for there is much more to be said about Jesus than that he is the Messiah. It will be one of the main questions the Church Fathers are to ask themselves individually: who do *you* think that I am? The Church will struggle for a while to answer that question more specifically and accurately. It will take more than eight generations of Church Fathers to clarify and explain the answer to the fullest, as we will see in the upcoming chapters.

After Jesus' death, his followers had to face another pivotal question: how would the world know that he, the Messiah, was ever here? How would his work be preserved and continued? The apostles and the other disciples would bring their new message to all the corners of the Roman Empire. They would spread this new religion, Christianity, to all Roman citizens, Jew or Gentile. Initially, Christianity was considered a small branch of Judaism and therefore would experience a rather tolerant treatment. But things would change soon. Suetonius, a non-Christian source about the Christians, refers to the expulsion of Jews by Emperor Claudius (41-54) and states, "Since the Jews constantly made disturbances at the instigation of Chrestus [sic], he expelled them from Rome."[25] There was trouble at the horizon.

Things would even change for the worst at the time of

---

[24] Mk. 8:29, Mt. 16:15
[25] The Lives of the Twelve Caesars, 25, on Claudius.

The First Christians: Keeping the Faith in Times of Trouble

Emperor Nero. In 64, a great fire destroyed a large section of Rome, and Nero, who was probably responsible for the blaze, pinned the arson on this new religious sect. He started the first great persecution of Christians in the Roman Empire. The apostles Peter and Paul were among the victims of this persecution. Only when Nero committed suicide in 68, could some calm set in again.

Tacitus, another non-Christian source about the Christians, also gave us some details from a non-Christian perspective about the person these Christians were named after: "Christus, from whom the name had its origin, suffered the extreme penalty during the reign of Tiberius at the hands of one of our procurators, Pontius Pilatus."[26] Tacitus also relates how Nero dealt with these Christians: "Covered with the skins of beasts, they were torn by dogs and perished, or were nailed to crosses, or were doomed to the flames and burnt, to serve as nightly illumination, when daylight had expired."

Who were these first Christians really, other than despised citizens? Paul gives us a good description:

> *Consider your own calling, brothers. Not many of you were wise by human standards, not many were powerful, not many were of noble birth. Rather, God chose the foolish of the world to shame the wise, and God chose the weak of the world to shame the strong, and God chose the lowly and despised of the world, those who count for nothing, to reduce to nothing those who are something, so that no human being might boast before God. It is due to him that you are in Christ Jesus, who became for us wisdom from God, as well as righteousness, sanctification, and*

---

[26] Annals 15:44.

redemption.[27]

That which set these Christians apart from other Roman citizens was not only their beliefs but also their way of life. They obviously lived as a minority in a pagan, non-Christian world—as strangers in a strange land. Around the year 50, imperial Rome was a "superpower," at the peak of its military, economic, and political might. The famous *Pax Romana* had been established. But the empire had also become under the influence of addiction to luxury and excess. Paul knew very well and first-hand in what kind of world his Christians had to live. He prays for the Philippians "that you may be blameless and innocent, children of God without blemish in the midst of a crooked and perverse generation."[28]

Besides, it was a world in which persecutions against Christians would flare up easily and repeatedly, sometimes locally, sometimes globally. Today's Christians in the Western world are not really familiar with persecutions, although they are certainly taking place in the Near East and other places nowadays. But even in the Western world, there might soon be a time that persecutions will occur again, albeit it not necessarily in a physical way. In this respect, the late Cardinal George of Chicago uttered some prophetic words: "I am (correctly) quoted as saying that I expected to die in bed, my successor will die in prison, and his successor will die a martyr in the public square. What is omitted from the reports is a final phrase I added about the bishop who follows a possibly martyred bishop: 'His successor will pick up the shards of a ruined society and slowly help rebuild civilization, as the church has done so often in human

---

[27] 1 Cor 1:26-30.
[28] Phil 2:15.

history.'"[29]

b. Trouble Within: Ebionism

The 1st generation of Christians had to deal with the first heresy in its history. As we discussed earlier, any heresy makes an exclusive choice: it picks and chooses—either-or. In this case the exclusive choice is based on the following question: are the real Christians Jews or are they Gentiles? Are the real Christians circumcised Jews or uncircumcised Gentiles? Is the real Christianity based on the Old Covenant, or on the New Covenant instead? The choice of heresies is either-or, but never both. For the heresy of Ebionism, the choice was exclusively for Jews, not Gentiles, for circumcised Jews, not uncircumcised Gentiles.

The term "Ebionism"[30] was used also by the people who were living in Qumran, as shown in the Dead Sea Scrolls. Among Christians, the term "the poor" was at first a common designation for all Christians—a reference to their material and voluntary poverty. But soon it became a "Judaizing" heresy that identifies Christians with Jews and makes Christianity a branch of Judaism. Consequently, one had to be a Jew to be a Christian. Ebionism, like all following heresies, chooses a half-truth, not the whole truth.

The tension had gradually been building up according to the Acts of the Apostles: "At that time, as the number of disciples continued to grow, the Hellenists complained against the Hebrews because their widows were being neglected in the daily distribution."[31] Who are these two groups? The Hellenists were not necessarily Jews from the diaspora, but

---

[29] The Cardinal's Column in Chicago Catholic, Oct. 21 – Nov. 3, 2012.
[30] Derived from a Hebrew word that means "poor."
[31] Acts 6:1

were more probably Palestinian Jews who spoke only Greek. The Hebrews, on the other hand, were Palestinian Jews who spoke Hebrew or Aramaic, but may also have spoken Greek. Both groups belonged to the Jewish Christian community in Jerusalem.

The first Christians, as described in the first chapters of the Acts of the Apostles, were actually all Jews either by birth or conversion, for which the biblical term "proselyte" is used, and referred to by historians as "Jewish Christians." According to the Catholic Encyclopedia, the English term "proselyte" occurs only in the New Testament where it signifies a convert to the Jewish religion[32], though the same Greek word is commonly used in the Septuagint, the Greek translation of the Old Testament, to designate a foreigner living in Palestine. Thus the term seems to have passed from an original local and chiefly political sense, in which it was used as early as 300 BC, to a technical and religious meaning in the Judaism of the New Testament era.

It is to be expected that this tension between the Old and New Covenant, between Jews and Gentiles in the Church, posed a danger to the unity of the Church—making for a potential schism—and a danger to her doctrine—making for a potential heresy. The heresy of Ebionism chooses the Old Covenant over the New Covenant, and the circumcised Jews over the uncircumcised Gentiles. Whoever chooses differently is rejected as a real and true Christian.

The Judaizing party of the Ebionists viewed Christianity just as God's final touch upon the masterpiece of Judaism. So they rejected Paul as an apostate to the Jewish Law, and they maintained there is no second, new Covenant, but only one

---

[32] Matthew 23:15; Acts 2:11; 6:5; etc.

The First Christians: Keeping the Faith in Times of Trouble

Old Covenant. They denied the Divinity and the virginal birth of Christ; they clung to the observance of the Jewish Law; they observed the Sabbath instead of the Sunday; they regarded Paul as a runaway, and used only one Gospel, the one according to Matthew. Most Christian sources portray the Ebionites as traditional Jews, who zealously followed the Law of Moses, revered Jerusalem as the holiest city, and restricted table fellowship to Gentiles only after they had converted to Judaism. Obviously, Ebionism was in essence a divisive movement: it separated Christians in two groups— Jews and non-Jews. Division is a serious threat to Christian unity: it creates a schism, even more so than a heresy.

Even if we consider Ebionites as merely traditional Jews, we have to realize they were not only different *de facto*, but they also wanted to separate themselves from other Christians for being different. In the books of the New Testament, the Ebionites are said to have accepted only a Hebrew (or Aramaic) version of the Gospel of Matthew, referred to as the Gospel of the Hebrews; they took it as an additional scripture to the Hebrew Bible. This version of Matthew, Irenaeus reports, omitted the first two chapters (on the nativity of Jesus), and started with the baptism of Jesus by John. So the Ebionites were not only "different," but they also believed that all Jews and Gentiles must observe the commandments in the Law of Moses.

The process of separation may have started rather inadvertently. It is most likely that, originally, the term "Ebionism" did not designate a heretical sect, but merely the orthodox Jewish Christians of Palestine, especially in Jerusalem, who continued to observe the Mosaic Law. The 5th generation Church Father Origen seems to confirm this: "those Jews who have received Jesus as Christ are called by the name of Ebionites."³³ A more moderate faction of the Ebionites, the so-called Nazarenes, claimed that only Jewish Christians must be circumcised and keep the Mosaic Law, but Gentile Christians need not.

However, these Judaizing Christians, ceasing to be in touch with the bulk of the Christian world, would gradually drift away from the standard of orthodoxy and become formal heretics. A stage in this development is seen in the writings of Justin, a 3rd generation Church Father, who speaks of two sects of Jewish Christians estranged from the Church: those who observe the Mosaic Law for themselves, but do not require observance thereof from others; and those who hold it of universal obligation. The latter are considered heretical, because they claim that one has to be or become a Jew if one wants to be or become a Christian.

Justin writes about this to a certain Trypho who seems to be a Judaizer, or at least lives among them:

> *But if some, through weak-mindedness, wish to observe such institutions as were given by Moses, from which they expect some virtue, but which we believe were appointed by reason of the hardness of the people's hearts, along with their hope in this Christ, and [wish to perform] the eternal and natural acts of righteousness and piety, yet choose to live with the Christians and the faithful, as I said before, not inducing them either to be circumcised like themselves, or to keep the Sabbath, or to observe any other such ceremonies, then I hold that we ought to join ourselves to such, and associate with them in all things as kinsmen and brethren. But if, Trypho, some of your race, who say they believe in this*

---

³³ Contra Celsum 2:1.

The First Christians: Keeping the Faith in Times of Trouble

> *Christ, compel those Gentiles who believe in this Christ to live in all respects according to the law given by Moses, or choose not to associate so intimately with them, I in like manner do not approve of them.*[34]

Because the heresy of the Ebionites chooses one half of the truth, there could be another heresy that chooses the other half of the truth— at the opposite end of the spectrum— which is, a bit later (mid-2nd century), the heresy of Marcion. Marcion believed Jesus was the savior sent by God, and Paul the Apostle was his chief apostle. He rejected the Hebrew Bible and the God of Israel. Marcion, and his Marcionites, believed that the wrathful Hebrew God was a separate and lower entity than the all-forgiving God of the New Testament. Marcion's Scriptural canon rejected the entire Old Testament, along with all other epistles and gospels of the twenty-seven books in the New Testament canon because they transmitted "Jewish" ideas. He did this in spite of the fact that Jesus himself had made very clear that he did not change one iota of the Jewish Law: "not the smallest letter [iota] or the smallest part of a letter will pass from the law, until all things have taken place."[35] Yet, Paul can say that Christ was "born under the law, to redeem those who were under the law."[36] Paul's epistles enjoy a prominent position in Marcion's canon since Paul is credited with correctly transmitting the gracious universality of Jesus' message in opposition to the harsh dictates of the "just god" of the Old Testament—but also in opposition to the God of Ebionism.

It shouldn't come as a surprise that the heresy of Ebionism would consider any influence of the Hellenistic Gentiles on

---

[34] Dialogue with Trypho 47.
[35] Mt. 5:18.
[36] Gal. 4:4-5.

Christianity as a distortion of its original purity. Judaizers criticize Christianity for having come under "Hellenistic influence." But interestingly enough, those who reject any "Hellenistic influence" in Christianity do not realize that their claim itself is a statement that "Judaizes." As Rod Bennett puts it: "the very phrase itself Judaizes; it assumes that Christianity is a Jewish thing being exported to Greeks—and that the Greek element is alien to it, something to be tolerated at best. And yet the New Testament is written in Greek, because it is for Greeks."[37] As a matter of fact, the early Gospel message was spread orally, probably in Aramaic, but almost immediately also in Greek. Hellenistic elements were an inevitable part of early Christianity.

c. Defenders of the Faith

Simon Peter (1-67)

After Jesus, Peter is the figure most frequently mentioned in the New Testament. It is 75 times that he is called *Simon*, which is the Greek version of his original Hebrew name *Simeon*. But he is also mentioned 154 times with the nickname *Petros*, "rock," which is the Greek translation of the Aramaic name Jesus gave him directly, *Cephas*. In the Old Testament, a change of name usually preceded the assignment of a mission. So when Simon was given a new name, that name was more than just a name, but a "mandate." But no matter how important Peter was for the Church, it is always Christ's Church, not Peter's. So thankfully, Scripture does not glorify Peter as a superhero, but portrays his weaknesses as well.

Simon Peter heads every New Testament list of apostles, which leaves no doubt that he was preeminent among the

---

[37] The Apostasy That Wasn't, p. 185.

Twelve. Luke tells us that after Jesus had called Peter, he embarked on his boat to address the people who had followed him.[38] At that moment, as Pope Benedict XVI put it, "the boat of Peter becomes the chair of Jesus,"[39] so that the chair or see of Peter can become the boat from which Jesus preaches. Of course, Jesus had more disciples than the Twelve. But somehow the Twelve have a special position and a special calling. It was custom of every rabbi to have five disciples, but Jesus went from five to twelve apostles, which shows us he was not one of those numerous rabbis; instead he had come to gather the twelve tribes of Israel. The Book of Revelation mentions, "The wall of the city had twelve courses of stones as its foundation, on which were inscribed the twelve names of the twelve apostles of the Lamb."[40]

Peter is one of the Twelve who were chosen and called by Jesus himself. There are no doubts about the historicity of this call. There are many witnesses to testify to this, but also for the simple reason that Judas, who betrayed him, is one of those called too, notwithstanding the difficulties that his presence could have caused the first Christians; he is repeatedly called "one of the twelve"—perhaps reluctantly, but historically correct. The Twelve Apostles are the most evident sign that between Christ and his Church there is no opposition. Despite the sins of the people who make up the Church, they are inseparable. Therefore, Christians cannot say "Yes" to Jesus, and "No" to his Church.

The Acts of the Apostles suddenly stops mentioning Peter after he was freed from prison: "Then he left and went to another place."[41] It does not tell us where "another place" is,

---

[38] Lk 5:1-3.
[39] 2007, 41.
[40] Rev. 21:14.
[41] Acts 12:17.

but Ignatius of Antioch, a Church Father of the 2nd generation, indicates that he ultimately went to Rome where he would be crucified during Nero's persecution (see 3.c). Several early sources record that when they heard about the events in Rome under Nero, Peter and Paul met in Corinth and agreed to leave for Rome immediately, so they could lend their combined support to the suffering flock who were dying at Nero's hand. According to the Church historian Eusebius, Paul was beheaded in Rome during Nero's reign. Peter is said to have died in 67 at the age of 66, also during the persecution by Nero.

Unfortunately, Luke's report in Acts, from chapter 13 on, shifts focus from Peter to Paul. The last chapter of Acts has Paul enter Rome, where he "was allowed to live by himself, with the soldier who was guarding him."[42] The Book of Acts was most likely finished before Nero's persecution began in 64-65. The earliest possible date for the composition of Acts is set by the events with which it ends, Paul's imprisonment in Rome around the year 63. The majority of scholars, however, date Acts to around 80, on the grounds that it uses Mark as a source and looks back on the destruction of Jerusalem in 70. We will leave this discussion for what it is.

So let's shift focus back to Peter's role in fighting the heresy of Ebionism. He was certainly not the one to lead this case. For Peter it was not easy to separate the Hebrew faith from the Hebrew culture he had been brought up with. He had always associated everything good and decent and godly with Israel and its religion, and everything lawless and superstitious with the paganism of the Greek and Roman world. He was probably not alone among the apostles.

---

[42] Acts 16 (Paul was a Roman citizen, which gave him certain privileges).

The First Christians: Keeping the Faith in Times of Trouble

However, it is worth noting that some of the apostles did not have a Hebrew but Greek name, which indicates Jesus had already a wider Church in mind; it was a sign of Jesus' cultural openness. Andrew and Philip, for instance, had Greek names, which was not uncommon in Galilee. Philip was probably able to speak Greek so he could be the interpreter for the Greeks who had come to Jerusalem for the Passover.[43] And Thomas, who had a Hebrew name, is sometimes called in John's Gospel "Didymus," another Greek name. In addition, Matthew was a tax collector for the Romans who had occupied Palestine. In other words, it was a rather "mixed" group.

What made things even more difficult for Peter is the fact that the first Christians and their Scriptures were keen to express that Jesus' mission was first and foremost to Israel and the Jews. Given Jesus' rather exclusive mission to Israel, it took a while for the Early Church, most notably for Peter, to recognize that salvation was also available to the Gentiles without converting to Judaism. Although the Jewish Christians who had fled the persecution in Jerusalem had gone into the Gentile regions of Phoenicia, Cyprus, and Antioch, they were still "spreading the word only among Jews.[44] Peter himself was rather hesitant to bring the Gospel to a Gentile household, but God made it clear to him that Cornelius was also one of the elect.[45]

What was Jesus' position in this debate? On the one hand, he tells us he was sent to the people of Israel first.[46] Jesus selected Jewish disciples, spoke in Jewish synagogues and the Jewish temple, and traveled mostly in Jewish areas. His

---

[43] Jn 12:20-22.
[44] Acts 11:19.
[45] Acts 10.
[46] Mt 10:5-6; Mt 15:24; Rom 1:16; Mk 6:34.

mission, in fulfillment of the Jewish prophets, was to the Jewish people. On the other hand, none of this means that Jesus' ministry was limited exclusively to the Jews. For instance, he does minister to the Gentiles at various occasions. He ministered to a Samaritan woman: "The woman was a Greek, a Syrophoenician by birth, and she begged him to drive the demon out of her daughter."[47] He spoke extensively with a Samaritan woman at the well.[48] He healed a Roman centurion's servant.[49] He traveled through the Gentile region of the Gerasenes.[50] And before his Ascension into Heaven, he sends his disciples on a mission with these words: "you will be my witnesses in Jerusalem, throughout Judea and Samaria, and to the ends of the earth."[51] No doubt, Israel has a special place in God's salvation, but not an exclusive one. It is Israel that God had prepared for the coming of the Messiah—indeed, "Salvation is from the Jews."[52] Paul, in his missionary journeys, followed the same priority of preaching to the Jews first.[53]

So was Ebionism right then in claiming that converted Gentiles should strictly follow the Law of Moses, should be circumcised, and should honor the Sabbath day instead of the Sunday? It took Peter a while to realize that he was dealing with a heresy here. It took actually a "dream" to make him go to the house of a Gentile, Cornelius, to whom he said, "You know that it is unlawful for a Jewish man to associate with, or visit, a Gentile, but God has shown me that

---

[47] Mk 7:24-30.
[48] John 4:4-42.
[49] Luke 7:1–10.
[50] Mark 5:1.
[51] Acts 1:8.
[52] Jn 4:22.
[53] Romans 1:16.

I should not call any person profane or unclean."[54]

But more was needed. The Acts of the Apostles reports, "Some who had come down from Judea were instructing the brothers, 'Unless you are circumcised according to the Mosaic practice, you cannot be saved.'"[55] They were preaching Ebionism! This convinced Paul that he had to go to Jerusalem. During the meeting there, "some from the party of the Pharisees who had become believers stood up and said, 'It is necessary to circumcise them and direct them to observe the Mosaic law.'"[56] Obviously, the Church had to make an official decision about this heresy, which she did during the first Church Council in Jerusalem.

After much debate had taken place at the Council, Peter got up and said to them,

> *My brothers, you are well aware that from early days God made his choice among you that through my mouth the Gentiles would hear the word of the gospel and believe. And God, who knows the heart, bore witness by granting them the holy Spirit just as he did us. He made no distinction between us and them, for by faith he purified their hearts. Why, then, are you now putting God to the test by placing on the shoulders of the disciples a yoke that neither our ancestors nor we have been able to bear? On the contrary, we believe that we are saved through the grace of the Lord Jesus, in the same way as they.*[57]

Acts tells us in detail what the Council did. The Apostle Peter

---

[54] Acts 10:28.
[55] Ibid. 15:1.
[56] Ibid. 15:50.
[57] Ibid. 15:7-11.

issued the basic decision.[58] Then the Apostles Paul and Barnabas gave supporting evidence: "The whole assembly fell silent, and they listened while Paul and Barnabas described the signs and wonders God had worked among the Gentiles through them."[59] Then the Apostle James proposed to make implementation of the decision easier: "It is my judgment, therefore, that we ought to stop troubling the Gentiles who turn to God, but tell them by letter to avoid pollution from idols, unlawful marriage, the meat of strangled animals, and blood."[60] The result was a circular letter: "we have with one accord decided to choose representatives and to send them to you along with our beloved Barnabas and Paul.[61] The letter they carried was in force for all Christian communities: "As they traveled from city to city, they handed on to the people for observance the decisions reached by the apostles and presbyters in Jerusalem.[62]

So, the Church had officially spoken. Their decision was based on what Jesus had told them and what the Holy Spirit had revealed to them. As said earlier (1.a), the apostles could not validate their decision by going back to the New Testament, for there was no New Testament yet, no Acts of the Apostles. The New Testament was still in the making, in the midst of the living Church.

Although technically Peter is not considered a Church Father, but an apostle, he was the first in line to guide the Church around the road blocks of heresies and schisms. The Twelve had been chosen and called, not to proclaim an idea,

---

[58] Ibid. 15:7-11.
[59] Ibid. 15:12.
[60] Ibid. 15:19-20.
[61] Ibid. 15:25.
[62] Ibid. 16:4.

but to witness to a person, Jesus Christ, and his message. But the cause was not going to end with them. The Twelve took pains to prepare successors, so that the mission entrusted to them would be continued after their death. Obviously, the Church Fathers would play an important role in this process.

Paul of Tarsus (5-67)

The first time the Acts of the Apostles mentions Paul—called Saul at the time—is at the stoning of Stephen, the first Christian martyr: "They threw him [Stephen] out of the city, and began to stone him. The witnesses laid down their cloaks at the feet of a young man named Saul.[63] It was then that Saul would hear how the first Christian martyr, Stephen, had to deal with the tension between the Law and Jesus, between the Old Covenant and the New Covenant:

> *Then they instigated some men to say, 'We have heard him speaking blasphemous words against Moses and God.' They stirred up the people, the elders, and the scribes, accosted him, seized him, and brought him before the Sanhedrin. They presented false witnesses who testified, 'This man never stops saying things against [this] holy place and the law.'*[64]

In his last discourse, before being stoned, Stephen actually interpreted the whole of the Old Testament in the light of Christ. He also showed them that the cult of the Temple was over and that Jesus, the Risen One, was the new, true "temple."

The killing of Stephen unleashed a local persecution of Christ's disciples, the first one in the history of the Church: "On that day, there broke out a severe persecution of the

---

[63] Ibid. 7:58
[64] Ibid. 6:11-13

church in Jerusalem, and all were scattered throughout the countryside of Judea and Samaria, except the apostles."[65] Apparently, Christianity had been spreading from Jerusalem to neighboring regions. So Saul was also expanding his persecution of Christians to other places, notably to Damascus. It was on his way to persecute Christians at Damascus that Jesus appeared to him and redirected his life: "On his journey, as he was nearing Damascus, a light from the sky suddenly flashed around him. He fell to the ground and heard a voice saying to him, 'Saul, Saul, why are you persecuting me?'"[66] In other words, in persecuting the Church, Paul was persecuting Christ. In his conversion, Paul was converted to Christ and to his Church.

Once a Christian, Paul started his travels in the Church of Antioch in Syria, where for the first time the Gospel was announced to the Greeks:

> *Now those who had been scattered by the persecution that arose because of Stephen went as far as Phoenicia, Cyprus, and Antioch, preaching the word to no one but Jews. There were some Cypriots and Cyrenians among them, however, who came to Antioch and began to speak to the Greeks as well, proclaiming the Lord Jesus.*[67]

Paul was more inclined than Peter to be the bridge builder between Judaism and Hellenism. Although he realized that Jesus' mission was first of all to the Jews, he also knew the focus was shifting. Together with Barnabas, Paul spoke boldly to the Jews: "It was necessary that the word of God be spoken to you first, but since you reject it and condemn

---

[65] Ibid. 8:1.
[66] Ibid. 9:4
[67] Ibid. 11:19-20

yourselves as unworthy of eternal life, we now turn to the Gentiles."[68]

Paul deeply believed Christ had commissioned him as an apostle to the Gentiles: "for the one who worked in Peter for an apostolate to the circumcised worked also in me for the Gentiles."[69] Although he had been a devoted Jew, even a former rabbi and Pharisee, it is striking that he would emerge as the enemy of Ebionism. Yet, Paul had discovered a new Faith that places not so much the Law of Moses at the center but rather the person of Jesus, Crucified and Risen: "a person is not justified by works of the law but through faith in Jesus Christ."[70] No wonder, in Paul's letters, after the Name of God, which appears more than 500 times, the name most frequently mentioned is Christ's—actually 380 times.

Once the Council of Jerusalem in 49 had officially declared Ebionism as a heresy, Paul would be very determined to enforce the new Christian doctrine. He would raise his voice when he noticed traces of Ebionism. The Council had not completely stopped Judaizing tendencies, so Paul was forced to combat Ebionism on several occasions, most notably in his epistles to the Galatians and the Romans.[71]

In his Letter to the Galatians, for instance, Paul tells us that in Antioch Peter once stopped eating with Gentiles in order to appease the sentiments of certain Jews visiting the city. This caused Paul to rebuke him publicly: "I said to Cephas in front of all, 'If you, though a Jew, are living like a Gentile and not like a Jew, how can you compel the Gentiles to live like

---

[68] Ibid. 13:46.
[69] Gal. 2:8
[70] Gal. 2:16
[71] Rom. 16:17-18.

Jews?'"[72] And later on, he would have to say something similar to the Judaizers in Rome: "Does God belong to Jews alone? Does he not belong to Gentiles, too? Yes, also to Gentiles, for God is one and will justify the circumcised on the basis of faith and the uncircumcised through faith."[73] Then he added emphatically: "For there is no distinction between Jew and Greek; the same Lord is Lord of all, enriching all who call upon him."[74]

Ironically, even Paul himself sometimes succumbed to the demands of Jewish Christians. When Paul wanted Timothy to accompany him on his mission, he had him circumcised: "On account of the Jews of that region, Paul had him circumcised, for they all knew that his father was a Greek."[75] Perhaps the clearest act of accommodation in Paul's career is the incident in Acts 21. James and the leaders at Jerusalem convince Paul to undergo Jewish purification rituals and have sacrifices offered at the Temple: "So Paul took the men, and on the next day after purifying himself together with them entered the temple to give notice of the day when the purification would be completed and the offering made for each of them."[76]

But even cases like these show how important unity is for Paul and how he values charity over division. Ebionism creates division, but sometimes charity is needed even more. Paul's main concern is to keep the Church united—both Christian Jews and Christian Gentiles—but without offending anyone. He hates those "who are disturbing you

---

[72] Gal. 2:14.
[73] Rom 3:29-30.
[74] Rom 10:12.
[75] Acts 16:3.
[76] Acts 21:26.

and wish to pervert the gospel of Christ,"[77] for they are corrupting the Gospel that Paul was trying to keep pure with grim determination. Just like the other apostles and the future Church Fathers, Paul is someone who passes on what he had received, which is ultimately coming from Jesus. He is a link in the chain that connects us with Jesus. In his own words, "For I handed on to you as of first importance what I also received: that Christ died for our sins in accordance with the scriptures; that he was buried; that he was raised on the third day in accordance with the scriptures; that he appeared to Cephas, then to the Twelve."[78]

Because any divisive force is an existential threat to Christianity, Paul detests division:

> *I urge you, brothers, in the name of our Lord Jesus Christ, that all of you agree in what you say, and that there be no divisions among you, but that you be united in the same mind and in the same purpose. For it has been reported to me about you, my brothers, by Chloe's people, that there are rivalries among you. I mean that each of you is saying, 'I belong to Paul,' or 'I belong to Apollos,' or 'I belong to Cephas,' or 'I belong to Christ.' Is Christ divided? Was Paul crucified for you? Or were you baptized in the name of Paul?*[79]

Paul was also very aware of the threats the Church would have to face for the times to come. He could foresee all the heresies coming from within the Church:

> *For the time will come when people will not tolerate sound doctrine but, following their own desires and insatiable curiosity,* will accumulate*

---

[77] Gal. 1:7.
[78] 1 Cor 15:3.
[79] 1 Cor 1:10-13.

teachers and will stop listening to the truth and will be diverted to myths.[80]

Didache (c. 75)

This is not the name of a Church Father but of a very old, early Christian document written by an anonymous author. In 1873, a monk in Istanbul happened to find in the library of his monastery an old dusty collection of ancient documents, copied and collected by an eleventh-century scribe called Leo. The collection included one particular text that the monk had never heard of, so he neglected it at first. But it soon became the highlight of his discovery—"The Teaching of the Lord According to the Twelve Apostles," which became quickly known by the Greek word for "teaching," *Didache*. It had been mentioned by several Church Fathers, but it had disappeared for almost thousand years, until 1873. Most scholars believe the text was composed not later than 90 and perhaps as early as 60.

The Didache[81] is mentioned by the Church historian Eusebius as the "Teachings of the Apostles." It is the oldest known written "catechism". It has three main sections dealing with Christian ethics, rituals such as baptism and Eucharist, and Church organization. The opening chapters describe the virtuous Way of Life and the wicked Way of Death. The Lord's Prayer is included in full. Fasting is ordered for Wednesdays and Fridays. Two primitive Eucharistic prayers are given.

It starts by contrasting a culture of life versus a culture of death. Thus it begins as follows:

> *There are two ways, one of life and one of death;*

---

[80] 2 Tim. 4:3-4.
[81] pronounced [dɪdəkeɪ] or [dɪdəki].

> *but a great difference between the two ways. The way of life, then, is this: First, you shall love God who made you; second, your neighbour as yourself; and all things whatsoever you would should not occur to you, do not also do to another.*[82]

And then it contrasts Christian commandments with the lifestyle of pagans:

> *And the second commandment of the Teaching; You shall not commit murder, you shall not commit adultery, you shall not commit pederasty, you shall not commit fornication, you shall not steal, you shall not practice magic, you shall not practice witchcraft, you shall not murder a child by abortion nor kill that which is begotten. You shall not covet the things of your neighbour, you shall not forswear yourself, you shall not bear false witness, you shall not speak evil, you shall bear no grudge. You shall not be double-minded nor double-tongued; for to be double-tongued is a snare of death. Your speech shall not be false, nor empty, but fulfilled by deed. You shall not be covetous, nor rapacious, nor a hypocrite, nor evil disposed, nor haughty. You shall not take evil counsel against your neighbour. You shall not hate any man; but some you shall reprove, and concerning some you shall pray, and some you shall love more than your own life.*[83]

The Didache repeats what Jesus has taught us. It also stresses that unity is needed to combat division in Christian communities: "You shall not long for division, but shall bring

---

[82] Didache 1:1.
[83] Ibid. 2:1.

those who contend to peace."[84]

Given the fact that Ebionism was threatening the Early Church, it is interesting to see in the Didache how Jewish-Christians saw themselves and how they adapted their Judaism to Gentile Christians, more so than any other book in the Christian Scriptures. One of the issues is on which day Christians come together—on Sabbath or on Sunday, the "Lord's Day"—and whether they go for sacrifice in the Temple or for the sacrifice of the Eucharist:

> *But every Lord's Day gather yourselves together, and break bread, and give thanksgiving after having confessed your transgressions, that your sacrifice may be pure."*[85] *The Letter to the Hebrews had said already, 'Every priest stands daily at his ministry, offering frequently those same sacrifices that can never take away sins. But this one offered one sacrifice for sins, and took his seat forever at the right hand of God.'*[86]

Not only does this show us that the Eucharist was at the center of Christian worship, but also that it was understood in terms of a sacrifice rather than a meal, and it was done on the Lord's day, not on the Sabbath. This is quite remarkable given the fact that the Didache is such an early document in Christianity.

But its early date is also the reason why the hierarchical structure of the Church has not been fully settled yet. Or reversed, because the structure of the Church is still unsettled, the document must be considered very old. How do we know that this structure was still in its infancy? One of

---

[84] Ibid. 4.
[85] Ibid. 14.
[86] Hebr. 10:11-12.

the reasons is that the local ministers of the Church mentioned are only bishops and deacons. Missing are the priests (presbyters). The bishops are clearly presbyter-bishops, as in the Pastoral Letters of Paul[87] and in Acts.[88] But when the 2nd generation Church Father Ignatius of Antioch wrote in 107, or at the latest in 117, the three orders of bishops, priests, and deacons were already considered essential to the Church in Syria, Asia Minor, and Rome (see 3.c).

As a side note, the English term "priest" derives from the Greek word "presbyter," but the translation of this word is very inconsistent. Sometimes it is translated as "elder," especially in Protestant translations—in spite of the fact that Timothy, who is called an "elder," actually was a young man. Why not call him or any other "elder" a "priest," which was originally a bishop-overseer. One of the oldest Catholic translations in English, the *Douai-Rheims Bible*, uses the term "priest," whereas one of the oldest Protestant translations in English, the *King James Version*, speaks of "elder," because the term "priest" had become too controversial after the Reformation. Clement, a 1st-century bishop of Rome, refers to the leaders of the Corinthian church in his Letter to Corinthians as bishops and presbyters interchangeably (see 3.c). The New Testament writers also use the terms "overseer" and "elder" interchangeably and as synonyms.

Soon after the Didache, the structure of the Church would become more settled. The same would hold for her praxis and liturgy. The Apostles' Creed, for instance, would begin to take form in the early 100s as a baptismal creed that was

---

[87] Phil 1:1.
[88] Acts 20:17.

used in Rome. The same could be said about the Eucharistic Prayers; they would soon become more structured. But at least we know that the Eucharistic Prayer was very essential to Christians, whether they were Jews or Gentiles, both united in one Church. The clearest indication is Paul's early reference to the key words of the Eucharistic Prayer:

> *For I received from the Lord what I also handed on to you, that the Lord Jesus, on the night he was handed over, took bread, and, after he had given thanks, broke it and said, 'This is my body that is for you. Do this in remembrance of me.' In the same way also the cup, after supper, saying, 'This cup is the new covenant in my blood. Do this, as often as you drink it, in remembrance of me.'* [89]

---

[89] 1 Cor 11:23-25.

3. The 2nd Generation (80-130)

a. Backdrop

After twenty-five years of relative peace since the suicide of Nero, persecution broke out again. In the year 81, a new tyrant had come to power by the name of Domitian. He was the first emperor to crown himself with the title "Lord and God" [*Dominus et Deus*] and to demand every citizen to refer to him that way, which meant that all who refused to do this, particularly the Christians, were considered atheists who had to be persecuted. His subjects were required to burn incense before his divine image. Refusing to do so was asking for trouble, to put it mildly. This led to a bloody persecution during the reign of Emperor Domitian (81-95), followed soon by another one under the reign of the Emperor Trajan (98-117).

The Roman Empire was bathing in paganism. Yet, many citizens did not believe anymore in a pantheon of various gods. Pliny the Younger, writing from Italy about the year 112, complains that Christianity had already become so popular that the pagan temples were nearly empty and it had become difficult to sell meat sacrificed to idols.[90] Romans had begun searching in the East for more exotic and more mysterious religions, ranging from Zoroastrianism to the cult

---

[90] Pliny the Younger, in a letter to Emperor Trajan (Epistles 10.96).

of Mithras. Sages from the East were offering them answers they could not find in pure paganism. So Rome had been inundated with various cults. Especially Eastern cults would find their way to Rome. It is in this strange mix of new religions that a very different kind of religion had emerged: Christianity—a religion preached by a fisherman, the foremost disciple of Jesus Christ.

Even during more peaceful times when persecutions were more sporadic and only local, Christians were frequently targeted. When a natural disaster occurred, people would look for what could cause the anger of the gods. Since Christians were known to refuse worshipping any god but their own, they were an easy target to be blamed as troublemakers who should be persecuted to appease "offended deities." This is what happened, for instance, around 110 in Antioch. Ignatius, the bishop of this dangerous sect of Christians, was apprehended and sentenced to fight wild beasts in Rome for the amusement of the crowds and the pleasure of the emperor himself (see 3.c).

In spite of these persecutions, the sociologist Rodney Stark estimates that the number of Christians was growing by approximately 40% a decade during the first and second centuries.[91] The historian Susan Tyler Hitchcock reports, "By the year 100, more than 40 Christian communities existed in cities around the Mediterranean, including two in North Africa, at Alexandria and Cyrene, and several in Italy."[92] This phenomenal growth rate forced Christian communities to adapt to changes in their communities and in the relationship with their political and socioeconomic

---

[91] Stark, Rodney (1996). *The Rise of Christianity: A Sociologist Reconsiders History*. Princeton University Press. p. 207.

[92] Hitchcock, Susan Tyler; John Esposito (2004). *Geography of Religion*. National Geographic Society.

environment. As the number of Christians grew, the Christian communities became larger, more numerous, and farther apart geographically. The passage of time also moved some Christians farther from the original teachings of the apostles, thus giving rise to teachings that were considered heterodox and sowing controversy and divisiveness within churches and between churches.

The Church had to face the fact that the direct links with Jesus from the past were gradually passing away, mostly taken "by force" during persecutions. So it was important, more than ever, to have new witnesses with a direct connection to these first links. It is the writings of three bishops—Clement of Rome, Ignatius of Antioch, and later Polycarp of Smyrna—that are particularly informative of dangerous administrative and doctrinal deviations that occurred twenty to forty years after the Church had lost Peter and Paul and the other apostles. This new generation of leaders reportedly still had known the apostles personally and had studied under them. Therefore, they are more specifically called the "Apostolic Fathers" among the Church Fathers.

What was it like to be a Christian under their leadership? Christians may not be "*of* the world," but they are still "*in* the world." Here is a priceless gem, the *Epistle to Diognetus*, which we are most fortunate to have as only one copy survived the centuries. We do not know who wrote it. It came from the second century. It was, like the New Testament, originally written in Greek. In this brief excerpt we have preserved a magnificent description of Christian living, of what life was like in the early church community:

> *They dwell in their own countries, but simply as sojourners. As citizens, they share in all things*

> *with others and yet endure all things as if foreigners. Every foreign land is to them as their native country, and every land of their birth as a land of strangers. They marry, as do all others; they beget children; but they do not destroy their offspring. They have a common table, but not a common bed. They are in the flesh, but they do not live after the flesh. They pass their days on earth, but they are citizens of heaven. They obey the prescribed laws, and at the same time surpass the laws by their lives. They love all men and are persecuted by all. They are unknown and condemned; they are put to death and restored to life. They are poor yet make many rich; they are in lack of all things and yet abound in all; they are dishonored and yet in their very dishonor are glorified. They are evil spoken of and yet are justified; they are reviled and bless; they are insulted and repay the insult with honor; they do good yet are punished as evildoers. When punished, they rejoice as if quickened into life; they are assailed by the Jews as foreigners and are persecuted by the Greeks; yet those who hate them are unable to assign any reason for their hatred. To sum it all up in one word—what the soul is to the body, that are Christians in the world.*[93]

Rodney Stark basically confirms this when he gives us a good description of what Christianity had to offer a pagan world:

> *To cities filled with the homeless and impoverished, Christianity offered charity as well as hope. To cities filled with newcomers and strangers, Christianity offered an immediate basis for attachment. To cities filled with orphans and widows, Christianity provided a new and*

---

[93] Epistle to Diognetus. The anonymous author is called *Mathetes*, which simply means "a disciple."

expanded sense of family. To cities torn by violent ethnic strife, Christianity offered a new basis for social solidarity. And to cities faced with epidemics, fire, and earthquakes, Christianity offered effective nursing services. ... For what they brought was not simply an urban movement, but a new culture capable of making life in Greco-Roman cities more tolerable.[94]

b. Trouble Within: Docetism

Heresies are usually not completely false, we found out. They have half-truths—otherwise they would not have a chance to occupy the Christian mind. The half-truth of Docetism[95] is that Jesus is indeed the Son of God, but then he cannot be completely human at the same time.

The former part was nothing new. The Christian belief that Jesus was not only the Messiah but also the Son of God can be found all over the New Testament. It is very prevalent in the most recent Gospel, John's; but even in the oldest Gospel, Mark's, we find this belief repeatedly proclaimed— for instance, at his baptism by John the Baptizer, "And a voice came from the heavens, 'You are my beloved Son; with you I am well pleased,'[96] and during the Transfiguration, "then from the cloud came a voice, 'This is my beloved Son. Listen to him.'"[97]

But the latter part of Docetism was the heretical part by denying not so much Christ's divinity as his true humanity. According to Docetism, Jesus was really a pure spirit, merely a ghost in the machine of a human body, which makes him in

---

[94] *The Rise of Christianity*, Princeton University Press, 1996, page 161.
[95] Pronounced as [dō-sē′tĭz′əm], [dō′sə-tĭz′əm].
[96] Mk 1:11.
[97] Mk 9:7.

essence a false messiah. It "spiritualizes" everything in Christianity. It lets Christians remain Christian while avoiding the "scandal of the Cross" and the "scandal of the Incarnation." For most Greeks and Romans, the Creator of the Universe cannot become a baby in a manger. And the Crucifixion was even worse a scandal. In the words of Paul, "we proclaim Christ crucified, a stumbling block to Jews and foolishness to Gentiles."[98]

Docetism was on the rise during the 2nd generation of Church Fathers. Its name is derived from the Greek word *dokesis*, "appearance" or "semblance", because Docetism teaches that Christ only "appeared" or "seemed" to be a man, to have been born, to have lived and suffered and died. Docetism seemed to be a perfect fit for the pagan mind of Roman citizens. Docetists are basically "illusionists," who thought they could come to a logical conclusion: since Jesus was the Son of God, and God is Spirit, and all flesh is irredeemably evil, Jesus had to be no more than a spirit himself. When the apostles thought they had walked and talked with Jesus, they had actually walked and talked with a mirage. This mirage could not possibly have suffered real pain, not even on the Cross. Jesus had only taken on the *appearance* of a man—a "make-believe" person. His life on earth and his suffering on the Cross were nothing but a divine stunt of playacting. Jesus' Body just looked like flesh but wasn't flesh.

There is some connection with Gnosticism (see 4.b), which would become rampant during the next generation of Church Fathers, but also with the previous, older heresy of Ebionism. Some of the followers of Docetism were coming from a Jewish or Judaizing background, which made it hard for them to accept that the eternal, invisible God could take

---

[98] 1 Cor. 1:23.

on human flesh himself. The main reason why the Jews had wished to kill Jesus was that, in calling God his Father, he had made himself equal with God. Docetists just couldn't cope with the idea of God becoming man. They could not possibly accept the sentence, "the Word was made flesh", in a literal sense. They could not accept that the Incarnation has logical consequences. If God truly became man and dwelt among us, it means he became a man with flesh and blood, including all the limitations of time and space associated with his earthly humanity.

Docetists deny not only that Jesus, being pure spirit, came into the flesh but also that he could suffer and entangle himself in filthy flesh. They referred to the Passion as "the mystical fiction of the Cross." Christ only *seemed* to suffer, either because he ingeniously and miraculously substituted someone else to bear the pain, or because the occurrence on Calvary was a visual deception. Consequently, they also denied the Resurrection, because Jesus had never really had a body to raise in the first place. Jesus' human form was considered a pure mirage. Jesus Christ is thought of more or less as a God descending to earth whose humanity is basically only a kind of clothing behind which God himself speaks and acts. The God of Docetism was not the God who, according to Paul, "sent forth his Son, born of woman."[99]

Perhaps Paul was reacting to the heresy of Docetism when he wrote, "For in him dwells the whole fullness of the deity *bodily.*"[100] Or when he said about Jesus, "though he was in the form of God, ... he humbled himself, becoming obedient to death, even death on a cross."[101] And John definitely refers

---

[99] Gal 4:4.
[100] Gal. 2:9.
[101] Phil. 2:6-8.

to the same heresy: "many false prophets have gone out into the world. This is how you can know the Spirit of God: every spirit that acknowledges Jesus Christ come in the *flesh* belongs to God."[102]

c. Defenders of the Faith

Clement of Rome (?-99)

In 1632, the Patriarch of Constantinople gave the king of England a precious gift—it was a copy of the fifth-century bound volume of the Bible called the *Codex Alexandrinus*. It also contained a special jewel: a letter from Clement of Rome to the Church in Corinth.

Who was this Clement? According to a Church Father of the 3rd generation, Irenaeus, Clement was the 4th pope, a Roman who had learned the faith from Peter and Paul during their final years in the Imperial City. The 4th generation Church Father Tertullian reported that Peter himself had consecrated Clement a bishop. There we see that vital link again, going back ultimately to Jesus.

The 5th generation Church Father Origen and the earliest Church historian Eusebius want us to believe that Clement of Rome is the same Clement mentioned by name in Paul's Letter to the Ephesians: "they have struggled at my side in promoting the gospel, along with Clement and my other co-workers."[103] Whether this identification is correct, we leave here undecided.

What we do know is that Clement of Rome is the same person other works refer to as "Pope Clement" or "Pope St. Clement I." He was the 4th pope (88-99)—after Peter (33-67),

---

[102] 1 Jn 4:1-2
[103] Phil. 4:3.

Linus (67-76), and Anacletus (76-88). We don't know much more about him, except for what he tells us in his only surviving letter addressed to the Corinthians. His letter may very well have been written before the year 70, because he refers to sacrifices still being offered in the temple in Jerusalem, which was destroyed in the year 70.

Why was Clement's letter to the Corinthians needed? The Christians in Corinth didn't have a good history. Earlier, Paul had warned them already for divisions in their midst. Now it was Clement's task to stop rebellion against the leaders in the Church of Corinth. First he makes the connection with Paul:

> *Take up the epistle of the blessed Apostle Paul. What did he write to you at the time when the gospel first began to be preached? Truly, under the inspiration of the Spirit, he wrote to you concerning himself, and Cephas, and Apollos, because even then parties had been formed among you. But that inclination for one above another entailed less guilt upon you, inasmuch as your partialities were then shown towards apostles, already of high reputation, and towards a man whom they had approved. But now reflect who those are that have perverted you, and lessened the renown of your far-famed brotherly love. It is disgraceful, beloved, yea, highly disgraceful, and unworthy of your Christian profession, that such a thing should be heard of as that the most steadfast and ancient church of the Corinthians should, on account of one or two persons, engage in sedition against its presbyters.*[104]

What was Corinth's main problem? Clement makes no bones

---

[104] Letter to the Corinthians 47.

about it: "sedition against its presbyters." A few members of the Christian community in Corinth wanted the Church to be a democracy, in which all rules, practices, rituals, and beliefs are to be decided by a majority vote among her members. Their new motto was: let the people of the Church—particularly the smart and progressive ones—band together in committees and choose new leaders for themselves. For don't we all have the right to attend the church of our choice? Clement seems to think differently:

> *Why are there strifes, and tumults, and divisions, and schisms, and wars among you? Have we not [all] one God and one Christ? Is there not one Spirit of grace poured out upon us? And have we not one calling in Christ? Why do we divide and tear in pieces the members of Christ, and raise up strife against our own body, and have reached such a height of madness as to forget that we are members one of another?*[105]

Sedition must be and can only be avoided by submission to the bishop who traces himself back to the apostles. For Clement it is important for the Church that her members submit themselves to the authority of the bishop:

> *You therefore, who laid the foundation of this sedition, submit yourselves to the presbyters, and receive correction so as to repent, bending the knees of your hearts. Learn to be subject, laying aside the proud and arrogant self-confidence of your tongue. For it is better for you that you should occupy a humble but honourable place in the flock of Christ, than that, being highly exalted, you should be cast out from the hope of His people.*[106]

---

[105] Ibid. 46.
[106] Ibid. 57.

The First Christians: Keeping the Faith in Times of Trouble

Why submission to the bishop-presbyter—and not to a democratically elected leader? Clement makes it very clear that the backbone of the Church is what we call *apostolic succession*. Although Clement does not use these two words, his letter has the earliest written reference to the idea of apostolic succession—without using those very exact words yet. "Apostolic succession" stands for the line of bishops stretching back to the apostles—an uninterrupted chain of connections with the apostles, and thus with Jesus. What makes this concept so important for the Church? Clement had no doubts about how to determine which was the true Church and which doctrines are the true teachings of Christ. The test was simple: just trace the apostolic succession of the claimants. The Church Fathers themselves, beginning with Clement, were links in that chain of succession, so they regularly appealed to apostolic succession as a test for whether Catholics or heretics had correct doctrine.

Clement's message to Corinth is definite: not committees or ringleaders decide the truth in the Church, but bishops as chains in the apostolic succession. To find out which authorities are reliable and which doctrines are true, there is this very simple test—the test of apostolic succession. That's why it is so important for Clement to keep the apostolic succession—the uninterrupted link with the apostles—effective and unbroken, not only now but also for the future:

> *Our apostles also knew, through our Lord Jesus Christ, that there would be strife on account of the office of the episcopate. For this reason, therefore, inasmuch as they had obtained a perfect fore-knowledge of this, they appointed those [ministers] already mentioned, and afterwards gave instructions, that when these should fall asleep, other approved men should succeed them in their ministry. We are of*

> *opinion, therefore, that those appointed by them, or afterwards by other eminent men, with the consent of the whole church, and who have blamelessly served the flock of Christ, in a humble, peaceable, and disinterested spirit, and have for a long time possessed the good opinion of all, cannot be justly dismissed from the ministry.*[107]

The notion of *apostolic succession* is vital for the Church. It protects her from division and heresies by keeping her in direct contact with the apostles, and ultimately and most importantly with Jesus. In the words of Pope Clement:

> *The apostles have preached the gospel to us from the Lord Jesus Christ; Jesus Christ [has done so] from God. Christ therefore was sent forth by God, and the apostles by Christ. Both these appointments, then, were made in an orderly way, according to the will of God. Having therefore received their orders, and being fully assured by the resurrection of our Lord Jesus Christ, and established in the word of God, with full assurance of the Holy Ghost, they went forth proclaiming that the kingdom of God was at hand. And thus preaching through countries and cities, they appointed the first fruits [of their labours], having first proved them by the Spirit, to be bishops and deacons of those who should afterwards believe.*[108]

Sometimes Clement talks only about bishops and deacons; at other times he also mentions presbyters. As we discussed already, the word "presbyter" is most likely the origin of the English word "priest." Yet, the translation of this word has become rather controversial; sometimes it is translated as

---

[107] Ibid. 44:1-2.
[108] Ibid. 42.

"elder," sometimes as "priest." The word "elder" is favorite among Protestant translators, but it is awkward to call the young Timothy an "elder," although he was not an "older man" at all, but one to whom Paul exhorted, "Let no one despise you because of your youth."[109]

So why not call Timothy a "priest"? The answer is most likely that the first Christians tried to avoid the word "priest" because of its association with the Jewish Temple where priests sacrificed animals. But in the New Testament, Jesus himself is described as the High Priest.[110] What the priests of the New Testament do during the Eucharist is standing in for the High Priest who made a sacrifice for us. Yet, strangely enough, modern Bible translations do use the word "priest" in the Old Testament—in which it has no historical or etymological root—but not in the New Testament—from which the word actually derives. So this makes one wonder why the Old Testament priesthood is translated with that word in English today, but not the New Testament priesthood.

As a matter of fact, the Catholic priesthood is a share in the priesthood of Christ and traces its historical origins to the Twelve Apostles appointed by Christ. Those apostles in turn selected other men to succeed them as the bishops (*episkopoi*, "overseers") of the Christian communities, with whom were associated presbyters (*presbyteroi*, "priests") and deacons (*diakonoi*, "servants"). As communities multiplied and grew in size, the bishops appointed more and more "presbyters" to preside at the Eucharist in place of the bishop in the multiple communities of each region. Today, the rank of "presbyter" is typically what one thinks of as a

---

[109] 1 Tim. 4:12.
[110] E.g. Hebr. 7:26.

priest, although technically both a bishop and a presbyter are "priests" in the sense that they share in Christ's ministerial priesthood and offer sacrifice to God in the person of Christ. However, at the time of Clement, the terms *episkopos* and *presbyteros* were still used interchangeably, but the term *episkopos* was applied to the leader of a local church. All bishops are priests, of course, but the leading priest is the bishop.

Back to Clement's letter. How was it received? The Corinthians not only heeded Clement's authority—although coming from Rome, it was a message going back to the apostles. They also continued to read his letter during their Sunday worship. They found the letter so important that they copied it and sent it all around the empire (that's why it has survived in Greek, Latin, Coptic, and Ethiopian). This also shows how the bishop of the church in Rome—where both Peter and Paul had been martyred and buried—was respected by churches outside Rome.

It certainly looks like Corinth had a serious problem with episcopal authority, but it didn't seem to have a problem with the heresy of Docetism, for Clement did not mention that heresy as being present in Corinth. While the heresy of Docetism was on the rise during this time period, it seems Corinth was spared of it. Although Clement never directly addresses Docetism, there is another letter that indirectly does. The so-called *Second Epistle of Clement* is found in two Greek manuscripts and in the Syriac manuscript of the authentic letter of Clement. However, the Church historian Eusebius, who is the first to mention it, is careful to remark that "it was not as well-known as the first Epistle, since ancient writers have made no use of it." In fact, it is neither a letter nor a formal epistle, but a homily or discourse which was read in the meetings of the faithful. And it is most likely not from Clement of Rome.

Here are two passages taken from this document that address the heresy of Docetism explicitly:

> *And let no one of you say that this very flesh shall not be judged, nor rise again. Consider in what [state] you were saved, in what you received sight, if not while you were in this flesh. We must therefore preserve the flesh as the temple of God. For as you were called in the flesh, you shall also come [to be judged] in the flesh. As Christ the Lord who saved us, though He was first a Spirit became flesh, and thus called us, so shall we also receive the reward in this flesh.*[111]

> *The church being spiritual, was made manifest in the flesh of Christ, signifying to us that if any one of us shall preserve it in the flesh and corrupt it not, he shall receive it in the Holy Spirit. For this flesh is the type of the spirit; no one, therefore, having corrupted the type, will receive afterwards the antitype. Therefore is it, then, that He says, brethren, 'Preserve the flesh,' that you may become partakers of the spirit.*[112]

Ignatius of Antioch (35-108)

The 2nd generation Church Father Ignatius was Peter's second successor as leader of the Church in Antioch. He was the "pilot" able to bring those on board safe to shore—not only when the sea was calm and the winds favorable, but most of all when the waves were raging and the passengers themselves in turmoil. He piloted his Church for over thirty years up to his final journey to martyrdom in Rome.

Around the year 107, Ignatius of Antioch was arrested,

---

[111] Second Letter of Clement 9.
[112] Ibid. 14.

brought to Rome by armed guards and eventually martyred there in the arena. During his long trip from Antioch to Rome, he was chained to a squad of soldiers—he called them "ten leopards," men who were brutal and crude. They marched him on foot, all the way in chains, across Asia Minor to the west coast of Turkey, where he was finally put on a ship that carried him to Rome where the wild beasts waited him. During this trip, his captors made rest stops in several towns along the way. Since there were no persecutions going on there, delegations of Christians could come to honor and encourage Ignatius. The seven brief letters he managed to finish before embarking the ship to Rome serve as his last will and testament.

On his journey to martyrdom, at Smyrna in modern-day Turkey, Ignatius was greeted by Polycarp, the bishop of Smyrna (see 4.c). They had both been disciples of John the Apostle. However, much younger than Ignatius, Polycarp belonged to the next generation of Church Fathers and was destined to outlive him by many years, but he would suffer a similar destiny: a martyrdom for Christ. At the reception in Smyrna was also a delegation of Ephesus, of Magnesia, and of Tralles—all cities on the west coast of modern-day Turkey.

When the welcome delay with Polycarp in Smyrna had come to an end, Ignatius had another stop, at Troas, one step closer to his martyrdom in Rome. He could write at least three more letters: one to the Philadelphians, one back to his grieving friends in Smyrna, and a personal one to his much younger friend Polycarp. What he made clear in all these letters is that he was going to die for a person, Jesus Christ, not an ideology. Neither was he going to die for a Docetic person who never really died. In his own words, "I undergo all these things that I may suffer together with Him."[113] It is in all his seven short letters that he calls Jesus Christ sixteen times "God" (*theos*).

Although his road to martyrdom is probably the most heroic part of his Christian life, his letters are an equally heroic testimony of his Christian Faith. They have at least two pivotal themes very dear to him: the unity of the Church and her battle against Docetism.

His first theme, the unity of the Church, goes back again to the theme of apostolic succession, like it did for Clement. But unlike Clement, he actually used that very expression when he speaks of "the successions of the bishops":

> *It is within the power of all, therefore, in every Church, who may wish to see the truth, to contemplate clearly the* tradition *of the apostles manifested throughout the whole world; and we are in a position to reckon up those who were by the apostles instituted bishops in the Churches, and [to demonstrate] the* succession *of these men to our own times. ... by indicating that tradition derived from the apostles, of the very great, the very ancient, and universally known Church founded and organized at Rome by the two most glorious apostles, Peter and Paul; as also [by pointing out] the faith preached to men, which comes down to our time by means of the* successions of the bishops.[114]

It is through the apostolic succession that all authority comes ultimately from Jesus, as his Truth is intended to be passed down—not voted up or down. As a matter of fact, in the Catholic Church, each one of her members is part of an

---

[113] Letter to the Smyrnaeans, 4.
[114] Against Heresies 3:3:1-2.

apostolic succession. Each of us can say we know someone who knew someone, who knew …, who knew someone who actually saw the Risen Christ. In Ignatius' words:

> *It is therefore befitting that you should in every way glorify Jesus Christ, who has glorified you, that by a unanimous obedience you may be perfectly joined together in the same mind, and in the same judgment, and may all speak the same thing concerning the same thing, and that, being subject to the bishop and the presbytery, you may in all respects be sanctified.*[115]

In most of his letters, Ignatius clearly distinguishes bishops, priests, and deacons—much more explicitly than Clement of Rome had done before him:

> *See that you all follow the bishop, even as Jesus Christ does the Father, and the presbytery as you would the apostles; and reverence the deacons, as being the institution of God. Let no man do anything connected with the Church without the bishop.*[116]

In a farewell letter which this early bishop and martyr wrote to his fellow Christians in Smyrna (today Izmir in modern Turkey), Ignatius made the first written mention in history of "the *Catholic Church.*" Thus, the second century of Christianity had scarcely begun when the name of the Catholic Church was already in use. Ignatius expresses very clearly that the unity of the *Catholic Church* is based on Jesus Christ and expressed in obedience to the bishop. And this, in turn, is based on the unity of the Church as expressed in the Eucharist:

---

[115] Letter to the Ephesians 2:2.
[116] Letter to the Smyrnaeans 8.

> *Let that be deemed a proper Eucharist, which is [administered] either by the bishop, or by one to whom he has entrusted it. Wherever the bishop shall appear, there let the multitude [of the people] also be; even as, wherever Jesus Christ is, there is the Catholic Church.*[117]

> *[C]ome together into the same place, let there be one prayer, one supplication, one mind, one hope, in love and in joy undefiled. There is one Jesus Christ, than whom nothing is more excellent. Therefore run together as into one temple of God, as to one altar, as to one Jesus Christ, who came forth from one Father, and is with and has gone to one.*[118]

Ignatius' second theme, the battle against Docetism, keeps coming back in all his seven letters. The bishop is deeply concerned about the devastating effects of this heresy, which teaches that Jesus was not truly human but that he only *seemed* to possess a body, to suffer, and to die. He actually connects Docetists to the Judaizers of Ebionism: "For if we still live according to the Jewish law, we acknowledge that we have not received grace."[119] Therefore, Ignatius speaks of Docetists as "monsters in human shape" and bids the faithful not only not to receive them but even to avoid meeting them, for they are in essence "godless men" and "unbelievers." Repeatedly he exclaims:

> *If, as some godless men, I mean unbelievers, say, He has suffered only in outward appearance, they themselves are nought but outward show. Why am I in bonds? Why should I pray to fight with wild beasts? Then I die for nothing, then I*

---
[117] Ibid. 8.
[118] Letter to the Magnesians 7.
[119] Ibid. 8.

would only be lying against the Lord.[120]

He minces no words in his rejection of Docetism. In this passage, he repeats the word "truly" at least five times:

> *Stop your ears, therefore, when any one speaks to you at variance with Jesus Christ, who was descended from David, and was also of Mary; who was* truly *born, and ate and drank. He was* truly *persecuted under Pontius Pilate; He was* truly *crucified, and [truly] died, in the sight of beings in heaven, and on earth, and under the earth. He was also* truly *raised from the dead, His Father quickening Him, even as after the same manner His Father will so raise up us who believe in Him by Christ Jesus, apart from whom we do not possess the true life.*[121]

Ignatius had learned from his own mentor, the Apostle John, the reality of the Incarnation: "And the Word became flesh and made his dwelling among us."[122] And: "every spirit that acknowledges Jesus Christ come in the flesh belongs to God, and every spirit that does not acknowledge Jesus does not belong to God. This is the spirit of the antichrist that, as you heard, is to come, but in fact is already in the world."[123] Ignatius saw clearly that if Jesus had no *real* flesh, then his crucifixion was also "make-believe," and so would be our salvation:

> *Now, He suffered all these things for our sakes, that we might be saved. And He suffered* truly, *even as also He* truly *raised up Himself, not, as certain unbelievers maintain, that He only seemed to suffer, as they themselves only seem to*

---

[120] Trallians 10; Ephesians 7 and 18; Smyrnaeans 1-6.
[121] Letter to the Trallians 9.
[122] Jn 1:14.
[123] 1 Jn 4:2-3

be [Christians].[124]

Docetism ignores the tension between the divine one who is invisible and the human one who made himself visible for us, between the divine one who cannot suffer and the human one who suffered for us:

> *Look for Him who is above all time, eternal and invisible, yet who became visible for our sakes; impalpable and impassible, yet who became passible on our account; and who in every kind of way suffered for our sakes.*[125]

In the following passage, Ignatius rejects both Ebionism, which still honors the Sabbath, and Docetism, which denies the reality of the resurrection:

> *If, therefore, those who were brought up in the ancient order of things have come to the possession of a new hope, no longer observing the Sabbath, but living in the observance of the Lord's Day, on which also our life has sprung up again by Him and by His death—whom some deny, by which mystery we have obtained faith, and therefore endure, that we may be found the disciples of Jesus Christ, our only Master—how shall we be able to live apart from Him, whose disciples the prophets themselves in the Spirit did wait for Him as their Teacher?*[126]

In this light, it becomes understandable why Ignatius also attacks Docetists regarding the Eucharist:

> *They abstain from the Eucharist and from prayer, because they confess not the Eucharist to be the flesh of our Saviour Jesus Christ, which*

---

[124] Letter to the Smyrnaeans 2
[125] Letter to Polycarp 3.
[126] Letter to the Magnesians 9.

suffered for our sins, and which the Father, of His goodness, raised up again.[127]

All the letters cited above were written during Ignatius' journey to be martyred in Rome. It was on his way to martyrdom that he gave all the Churches along his way his last "will"—a message about unity, obedience, and orthodoxy. His way to Rome only made sense if Jesus' suffering was as real as his own suffering was.

As Pope John Paul II would later say about martyrs:

> *The martyrs know that they have found the truth about life in the encounter with Jesus Christ, and nothing and no-one could ever take this certainty from them. Neither suffering nor violent death could ever lead them to abandon the truth that they have discovered in the encounter with Christ.*[128]

---

[127] Letter to the Smyrnaeans 7.
[128] Encyclical *On Faith & Reason.*

4. The 3rd Generation (130-180)

a. Backdrop

To some extent, things were changing at the Imperial Court. For the next forty years (138-180), the emperor's throne would be occupied by Antoninus Pius (138-161) followed by his adopted son Marcus Aurelius (161-180). They were dedicated philosophers, schooled in Stoicism—with its insistence on patience, resignation, and virtue. These ideals would thoroughly transform the entire Imperial Court; the orgies, the intrigue, and the excess of earlier years at the Court would be banished. One of the most peaceful and prosperous times were ahead for a change—at least for most citizens, and for a rather short period of time. However, Nero's sixty-year old edict of "Christians no more" [*Christiani non sint*] was still left in place, albeit not heavily enforced, or imposed only locally by zealous governors.

What did not change, though, is that there were again periodic bloody persecutions for Christians during the reign of emperors Antoninus Pius and Marcus Aurelius. What was happening at the end of the second century is well put by the 4th generation Christian apologist (literally, "defender" of the faith) Tertullian (see 5.c). He complained about the widespread perception that Christians were the source of all disasters brought against the human race by the gods:

> *They think the Christians the cause of every public disaster, of every affliction with which the people are visited. If the Tiber rises as high as the city walls, if the Nile does not send its waters up over the fields, if the heavens give no rain, if there is an earthquake, if there is famine or pestilence, straightway the cry is, 'Away with the Christians to the lion!'*[129]

Perhaps one of the most popular sites in the Imperial City of Rome was the Flavian Amphitheater, better known as *The Coliseum* (or *Colosseum*). It was the fabulous sports and entertainment complex where thousands of Romans would crowd together on Sundays to be appeased with "bread and games" [*panem et circenses*]—with politicians giving out cheap food and entertainment to keep themselves in power. Every Sunday the growing crowd looks down in anticipation onto the arena floor, waiting for men or beasts to be released into the arena. A spectacle to behold! Even more so when Christians appear on the arena floor. Many of them were bound for Rome to be devoured by the beasts, for the amusement of the people.

But not all was "bread and games" in the Roman Empire. After *Pax Romana* had reigned for more than hundred years over the Mediterranean world, enforced by the incomparable power of the Roman military machine, barbarians were waiting at the frontiers of the Roman Empire to strike. No matter what Emperor Marcus Aurelius tried, the effect was useless—he was a Stoic philosopher, not a strong ruler. But military failure was not the only cause of decline. Perhaps a more important factor in Rome's gradual breakdown was a rapid decay of morality. It would usher in the beginning of the end for the Roman Empire. Justin, a Church Father

---

[129] The Apology 40.

living during this era (see 4.c), gave us a good description of what was happening in Roman society:

> [W]e see that almost all so exposed (not only the girls, but also the males) are brought up to prostitution. And as the ancients are said to have reared herds of oxen, or goats, or sheep, or grazing horses, so now we see you rear children only for this shameful use; and for this pollution a multitude of females and hermaphrodites, and those who commit unmentionable iniquities, are found in every nation. And you receive the hire of these, and duty and taxes from them, whom you ought to exterminate from your realm. And any one who uses such persons, besides the godless and infamous and impure intercourse, may possibly be having intercourse with his own child, or relative, or brother. And there are some who prostitute even their own children and wives, and some are openly mutilated for the purpose of sodomy; and they refer these mysteries to the mother of the gods, and along with each of those whom you esteem gods there is painted a serpent, a great symbol and mystery.[130]

Because of all that was happening to society, traditional sources of meaning and purpose had lost their lure. Many Romans had already given up their faith in the Greek and Roman gods. The gods they had heard about since childhood were simply human beings writ large. Many Romans had become agnostics, or were more interested in the god of philosophers. Even the emperor himself did no longer believe that Caesar is divine. Burning incense to the emperor had become a civic duty, something akin to the pledge of allegiance to the flag.

---

[130] First Apology 27.

With immorality spreading like wildfire in the Roman Empire, Christians became even more "outlandish." They were living like strangers in a strange land. They were living in a world of abortion, infanticide, sexual confusion, promiscuity, abuse of power, and exploitation of the poor. No wonder they were being charged with serious "crimes"—with atheism, incest, and cannibalism. It is certainly a delicate balancing act to be in the world but not of it.

Paradoxically, it is in this environment that the Christians of the 3rd century express their religion and seem to fill a gap that others are experiencing. They seem to have a religion that appeals to the growing group of agnostics among the heathens. It is on this curiosity that the philosophers among the Christians try to capitalize. The most illustrious example of them is the 3rd generation Church Father Justin. He talks to his fellow-citizens in a language they understand best. He tells them how different the morality of Christians is from the surrounding culture and from the aberrations they are accused of:

> *And on the day which is called Sunday there is an assembly in the same place of all who live in cities or in country districts; and the records of the apostles, or the writings of the prophets, are read as long as we have time [...] Sunday is the day on which we all hold our common assembly, because it is the day on which God, when he changed the darkness and matter, made the world; and Jesus Christ our Savior on the same day rose from the dead.*[131]

So it is not surprising that more and more Romans are intrigued by who these Christians are. What many people associate with this era of the Roman Empire are the

---

[131] Apologies 1:67.

catacombs. Were they still hiding places where Christians could hide for their enemies? Not really. What did the early Christians actually do in the catacombs? It was not so much a place to hide as a sanctuary for them to venerate the martyrs who had been persecuted: their icons, their examples, their role-models—in short, their Saints.

One of the greatest icons of this generation was the Church Father Polycarp, who was hauled from his bishop's see in Smyrna to Rome in order to be martyred there—very similar to what had happened to his older friend Ignatius of Antioch. Within months of Polycarp's death, the Church of Smyrna published an account of his martyrdom as a circular letter to the entire Catholic Church, commonly known as *The Martyrdom of Polycarp*. This document also relates how Polycarp's relics were deposited "in a fitting place"—perhaps a catacomb:

> *The centurion then, seeing the strife excited by the Jews, placed the body in the midst of the fire, and consumed it. Accordingly, we afterwards took up his bones, as being more precious than the most exquisite jewels, and more purified than gold, and deposited them in a fitting place, whither, being gathered together, as opportunity is allowed us, with joy and rejoicing, the Lord shall grant us to celebrate the anniversary of his martyrdom, both in memory of those who have already finished their course, and for the exercising and preparation of those yet to walk in their steps.*[132]

b. Trouble Within: Gnosticism

In the 2nd century "laboratory" of old and new philosophies, as sketched above, a new concoction was born. It was called

---

[132] The Martyrdom of Polycarp 18.

Gnosticism. No matter how bad the persecutions were for the 3rd generation of Christians, the worst calamity for the Church came from within: a new heresy, with a long-lasting impact on the history of the Church.

In times of uncertainty and gloominess, people often look for something new and exciting. And lo and behold, something new was brewing: a mixture of ideas drawn from Persia, ancient Oriental religions, Greek philosophy, sorcery, and other mysterious cults. This potion became known as *Gnosticism*. It was an eclectic movement generated out of a general experience of profound malaise in a dying culture. Similar to what we experience nowadays with ideas under the label of "New Age," Gnosticism was not an organized religion either but rather a general way of thinking and believing. But in reality, it turned all beliefs "upside down," so that what had been revelatory and sacred before now became negative and evil.

Gnosticism is a complex phenomenon; it incorporates several philosophies, but also previous heresies such as Ebionism and Docetism. Therefore, there are many diverse elements in Gnosticism. Probably its main element is its separation of the spiritual world from the material world. The material world is not seen as something "good" but rather as a horrible mistake, created by a lower spiritual being called the "Demiurge." Sparks of some spiritual realities managed to get trapped in human bodies. Since matter and spirit are utterly opposed, spirits need to be freed from the body and return to their heavenly home. This redemption is only possible, not through sacrifice, but through *gnosis*—the Greek word for "knowledge"—which supposedly brings us the liberating knowledge of our true origin.

The First Christians: Keeping the Faith in Times of Trouble

The way Gnostics think about the world has consequences for the way they think about humanity. Because Gnostics recognize a sharp contrast between the inferior, finite world of matter and the transcendent, spiritual realm of the divine, they also have an understanding of the human being that sharply divides the material or bodily, on the one hand, and the spiritual or mental or affective, on the other. For Gnostics, it is the immaterial, the mental, and the sentimental that ultimately count. They understood humans to represent sparks of the divine, but imprisoned in material bodies.

Another element in Gnosticism is its link with Ebionism, which separates the Old Testament from the New Testament. Gnostics opposed the God of the Old Testament, for he is the God who created Nature and promulgated the Law, the God who created human beings male and female and told them to be fruitful and multiply, the God who warned human beings that, although their freedom was wide-ranging, this freedom had to stop short of trying to take control over good and evil. None of this can be true for Gnostics: God is in his remote Heaven, far away from filthy flesh.

This reminds us also of the heresy of Marcion who held there are two very different Gods: the God of the Old Testament and the God of the New Testament. The God of the Old Testament was the evil Demiurge, so Marcion rejected the first "God" and the Old Testament, and truncated the New Testament to one Gospel, Luke's. Everything else had been inserted later, by some "heretics" working for the evil Demiurge. Only Gnostics knew the "real God."

A third element is the link between Gnosticism and Docetism. Gnosticism is Docetism taken to its extreme. In this view, it is impossible for the "Word" to become "flesh," as it says in John 1:14, for spirit and matter are totally antagonistic. Therefore, Gnosticism happily embraces Docetism in a perfect match: Jesus just *appeared* to be human. Therefore, Jesus did not suffer under Pontius Pilate; he was not crucified and was not raised on the third day. These things could not have really happened, for that would mean, according to Gnostics, that Jesus of Nazareth was human, actually too human. The Gnostic heresy proposed a Jesus detached from his humanity instead.

In Catholic theology, there is definitely a tension, a contrast, even a paradox in Jesus' life. Pope Benedict XVI sketched this as follows: "If we only proclaim Jesus' heavenly dimension, we risk making him an ethereal and evanescent being; and if, on the contrary, we recognize only his concrete place in history, we end by neglecting the divine dimension that properly qualifies him."[133] Jesus is not either God or man but he is both true God and true man. Choosing either side exclusively makes for a heresy. Gnosticism ends up with the ethereal and evanescent part of Jesus. That's why Gnosticism is a heresy. In the words of Russell E. Saltzman:

> *Gnosticism has never liked a historical Jesus rooted to a dusty land, who had to wash his own feet. It is embarrassed by the scandal of the particularity of Jesus, by his sheer Jewishness. It is embarrassed by suffering, by death. It is embarrassed by all the physical stuff it takes to live. It does not believe that divinity would ever mix it up with flesh and blood, even if it could.*[134]

A fourth element of Gnosticism is its condescending separation between the Gnostics and the masses, similar to the way the Judaizing version of Ebionism distinguished

---

[133] General Audience on Wednesday, 4 October, 2006.
[134] First Things 3.10.16.

Jewish Christians from Hellenistic Christians. The Gnostics considered themselves blessed with the real "gnosis" that no one else had. Those who had attained higher levels of spiritual "knowing" and whose ascetic practices had refined their bodies into perfect temples of "the spirit," were an "elite" who could look with a sad disdain at the great unwashed, those still tied to bodies and matter and nature.

A fifth element of Gnosticism is its exclusive access to a secret tradition going back to Jesus himself. Jesus must have known that most Christians could not handle his true teaching, so he *secretly* entrusted it to a few elite confidants. Gnostics represent themselves as "improvers of the apostles," in the words of a Church Father of this generation, Irenaeus (see 4.c). Improvement was badly needed, for these simple fisherman were just plain, unlettered laborers who were unable to grasp fully the subtleties of their Teacher's message. The apostles which Jesus had chosen were basically declared simpletons. Gnostics, however, were given "later and fuller" revelations passed down by Peter or Paul in *secret*. God had a secret, which was disclosed, and then only in part, to certain "knowers"—prophets and apostles. It is this secret knowledge that separates the initiated from the masses.

A sixth element of Gnosticism is that Gnostics are all intent to go ahead with their private interpretations without any oversight by bishops, who were once thought to be the living link with Jesus Christ himself. They were sure the Apostolic Church had gotten it wrong. They considered the Church to be mere flesh, so people need only the Holy Spirit to guide them in interpreting the Scriptures and Christian faith and doctrine. In short, Gnosticism seeks private spirituality without sacrifice, without authority, without the Cross.

Gnosticism may seem an old philosophy and heresy, but it is still very much alive in our modern times. We find it again in the occult "New Age" spirituality and in movies and books such as *The Da Vinci Code*. It also reemerged, for instance, when people started to declare that the soul actually lives in the prison of the body, waiting anxiously to be released. This false belief makes some people decide to undergo sex-change surgery because they had the feeling that their soul was "trapped" in the body of the opposite sex. Cases like these set the soul in opposition to the body, based on the mistaken Gnostic belief that only the soul is considered the "real me," thus leaving the body at the mercy of the soul. In this view, an entirely isolated soul can decide on its own what the body should be, male or female—as if it were a merely material vehicle. The truth is that our bodies are us. When our bodies ail, we ail; when they fail, we fail. However, as Robert George says, "The idea that human beings are non-bodily persons inhabiting non-personal bodies never quite goes away."[135] Ideas like this are in essence modern versions of Gnosticism.

c. Defenders of the Faith

Polycarp of Smyrna (69-155)

Polycarp could be called the most well-connected bishop in the ancient Church. He was a young disciple of the Apostle John, became later a bishop-colleague of Ignatius of Antioch, and finally tutored a young man who would grow up to be another Church Father, Irenaeus, bishop of Lyons. What united them was the fact that Polycarp and the other Fathers of this generation had personally known the men who had been with Jesus—and that makes all the difference in the world.

---

[135] *First Things* 12-2016.

The First Christians: Keeping the Faith in Times of Trouble

Polycarp was a close friend of Ignatius, although he was much younger—that's why we list him with the third generation of Church Fathers. Polycarp was a relatively young bishop at the time he met Ignatius who was on his road to Rome to be executed. Of Ignatius's seven letters, only one was addressed not to a Church but to an individual, Polycarp.

Forty years after the encounter of Ignatius and Polycarp, a local persecution was flaring up again—this time in Smyrna, present-day Turkey. One day, when a Christian youth in the amphitheater of Smyrna encouraged the beasts to devour him, the crowd went berserk and began to chant, "We want Polycarp! We want Polycarp!" Now it was Polycarp's turn to become the next target for martyrdom. Eyewitnesses report his martyrdom, while the crowd in the stadium was shouting "Away with the Atheists":

> *[Polycarp] was conducted to the stadium, where the tumult was so great, that there was no possibility of being heard. ... But Polycarp, gazing with a stern countenance on all the multitude of the wicked heathen then in the stadium, and waving his hand towards them, while with groans he looked up to heaven, said, Away with the Atheists. Then, the proconsul urging him, and saying, Swear, and I will set you at liberty, reproach Christ; Polycarp declared, Eighty and six years have I served Him, and He never did me any injury: how then can I blaspheme my King and my Saviour?*[136]

That was the end of a very productive life—a life that saved the Church from going astray. Earlier in life, for instance, Polycarp had gone to Rome to fight against various heresies

---

[136] The Martyrdom of Polycarp 8-9.

that were present there. Apparently he had heeded what Ignatius had told him in his Letter to Polycarp:

> *Let not those who seem worthy of credit, but teach strange doctrines, fill you with apprehension. Stand firm, as does an anvil which is beaten. It is the part of a noble athlete to be wounded, and yet to conquer. And especially, we ought to bear all things for the sake of God, that He also may bear with us. Be ever becoming more zealous than what you are. Weigh carefully the times. Look for Him who is above all time, eternal and invisible, yet who became visible for our sakes; impalpable and impassible, yet who became passible on our account; and who in every kind of way suffered for our sakes.*[137]

We know most about Polycarp from others—from his contemporary, Irenaeus, and from Church historian Eusebius—but we do have a letter that he wrote himself to the Philippians. In this letter he is a strong advocate against the errors of Docetism and Gnosticism:

> *For whosoever does not confess that Jesus Christ has come in the flesh, is antichrist; and whosoever does not confess the testimony of the cross, is of the devil; and whosoever perverts the oracles of the Lord to his own lusts, and says that there is neither a resurrection nor a judgment, he is the first-born of Satan. Wherefore, forsaking the vanity of many, and their false doctrines, let us return to the word which has been handed down to us from the beginning.*[138]

We have no other letters from Polycarp, but we do know from the Church historian Eusebius how unwavering

---

[137] Letter to Polycarp 3.
[138] Letter to the Philippians 7.

Polycarp was regarding heretics. He was appalled at the Gnostic heretics he encountered in his old age. Eusebius describes this with the following words:

> [I]f that blessed and apostolic presbyter [Polycarp] had heard any such thing, he would have cried out, and stopped his ears, and as was his custom, would have exclaimed, 'O good God, unto what times have you spared me that I should endure these things?' And he would have fled from the place where, sitting or standing, he had heard such words.[139]

According to Eusebius, Polycarp was equally unyielding against the heretic Marcion:

> Polycarp himself, when Marcion once met him and said, 'Do you know us?' replied, 'I know the first born of Satan.' Such caution did the apostles and their disciples exercise that they might not even converse with any of those who perverted the truth.[140]

Polycarp felt very strongly, according to Eusebius, that he stood in the tradition of the apostolic succession. He knew that unity would only be possible by clinging rigidly to the principle of discipleship through an authentic link with previous witnesses:

> But Polycarp also was not only instructed by the apostles, and acquainted with many that had seen Christ, but was also appointed by apostles in Asia bishop of the church of Smyrna. We too saw him in our early youth; for he lived a long time, and died, when a very old man, a glorious and most illustrious martyr's death, having

---

[139] Church History 5:20:7.
[140] Ibid. 4:14:7.

always taught the things which he had learned from the apostles, which the Church also hands down, and which alone are true.[141]

His student, Irenaeus, also has only words of praise for Polycarp, especially in his fight against heresies:

But Polycarp also was not only instructed by apostles, and conversed with many who had seen Christ, but was also, by apostles in Asia, appointed bishop of the Church in Smyrna, whom I also saw in my early youth, for he tarried [on earth] a very long time, and, when a very old man, gloriously and most nobly suffering martyrdom, departed this life, having always taught the things which he had learned from the apostles, and which the Church has handed down, and which alone are true. To these things all the Asiatic Churches testify, as do also those men who have succeeded Polycarp down to the present time,— a man who was of much greater weight, and a more steadfast witness of truth, than Valentinus, and Marcion, and the rest of the heretics. He it was who, coming to Rome in the time of Anicetus caused many to turn away from the aforesaid heretics to the Church of God, proclaiming that he had received this one and sole truth from the apostles—that, namely, which is handed down by the Church.[142]

Polycarp's name was very appropriate, for "polycarp" means "much fruit" in Greek. With Clement of Rome and Ignatius of Antioch, Polycarp is regarded as one of three chief Apostolic Fathers. He was bishop of an important congregation which was a large contributor to the founding of the Christian Church. His role was to authenticate

---

[141] Ibid. 4:14:3-4.
[142] Against Heresies 3:3:4.

orthodox teachings through his reputed connection with the apostle John—he might even have been the angel of the church in Smyrna that the Book of Revelation refers to.[143] He was a spiritual giant. Even the soldiers who arrested him, after they heard him pray—and after he had made them a meal—regretted that they had been sent to arrest "so godly and venerable an old man."

Justin Martyr (100-165)

While other early Church Fathers like Ignatius and Polycarp wrote theology for Christians, Justin wrote philosophy tailored to pagans and Jews. At an early age, Justin was inspired by the old Greek philosopher Socrates. Socrates had been accused of rejecting pagan idolatry in his search for the one true God. Four centuries later, Justin would be trying to continue, and finally complete, this search. In fact, he actually followed also in the footsteps of the Apostle Paul, who around 51 went to Athens where he still found idols everywhere, but also an opening for Christianity: "For as I walked around looking carefully at your shrines, I even discovered an altar inscribed, 'To an Unknown God.' What therefore you unknowingly worship, I proclaim to you."[144] Paul even quoted some of their own poets in his speech on the Areopagus in Athens: "For 'In him we live and move and have our being,' as even some of your poets have said, 'For we too are his offspring.'"[145]

Like Paul, Justin engaged his pagan adversaries on common ground—philosophy—for he was convinced that a well-developed presentation of Christian Faith would win all thinking persons to Christ. So he referred his audience of

---

[143] Rev. 2:8.
[144] Acts 17:23.
[145] Acts 17:28.

philosophers to their icon Socrates:

> *And those who by human birth were more ancient than Christ, when they attempted to consider and prove things by reason, were brought before the tribunals as impious persons and busybodies. And Socrates, who was more zealous in this direction than all of them, was accused of the very same crimes as ourselves. For they said that he was introducing new divinities, and did not consider those to be gods whom the state recognised.*[146]

Although initially a pagan philosopher himself, Justin's eyes had been opened by the lifestyle and courage of the Christians he saw around him:

> *For I myself, too, when I was delighting in the doctrines of Plato, and heard the Christians slandered, and saw them fearless of death, and of all other-things which are counted fearful, perceived that it was impossible that they could be living in wickedness and pleasure. For what sensual or intemperate man, or who that counts it good to feast on human flesh, could welcome death that he might be deprived of his enjoyments, and would not rather continue always the present life, and attempt to escape the observation of the rulers; and much less would he denounce himself when the consequence would be death?*[147]

His dialogue with philosophy had begun—at the interface of Christianity and philosophy. Justin took up the ministry pioneered by Paul. He would wear—for the rest of his life, even as a Christian—the distinctive outfit [*pallium*] of a

---

[146] Second Apology 10.
[147] Ibid. 12.

philosopher. Around 150, he moved to Rome and opened a school of philosophy. As a Christian philosopher, he debated with Roman philosophers, Jewish rabbis, and heretics, inviting them to come to the full knowledge of the truth. Thus, he acted like a Platonist to the Platonists, a Stoic to the Stoics, and a Pythagorean to the Pythagoreans:

> *For while we say that all things have been produced and arranged into a world by God, we shall seem to utter the doctrine of Plato; and while we say that there will be a burning up of all, we shall seem to utter the doctrine of the Stoics: and while we affirm that the souls of the wicked, being endowed with sensation even after death, are punished, and that those of the good being delivered from punishment spend a blessed existence, we shall seem to say the same things as the poets and philosophers.[148]*

What then made him differ as a Christian philosopher from the Greek philosophers? It is, he said, the difference between partial truth and full truth. Justin considered the *full* truth a property of Christians:

> *I confess that I both boast and with all my strength strive to be found a Christian; not because the teachings of Plato are different from those of Christ, but because they are not in all respects similar, as neither are those of the others, Stoics, and poets, and historians.[149]*

In other words, he became a Christian *apologist*, a defender of the Christian faith—not to be misunderstood as someone who makes an "apology" (far from that). However, we don't remember him only as "Justin the Apologist" but also as

---

[148] First Apology 20.
[149] Second Apology 13.

"Justin the Martyr." Being an apologist was the reason why he became a martyr. Justin himself had predicted this; he had learned from Socrates what was ahead of people in search of truth in a pagan society: "I too, therefore, expect to be plotted against and fixed to the stake."[150]

Marcus Aurelius, a philosopher like Justin, would become emperor in 161. He also would always wear his distinctive "pallium." However, one of his first official acts as emperor was to issue an edict to banish sects or religions whose true nature is unknown. This edict would usher in a new round of persecution—the fourth one in the Church's history. And the most famous victim would be Justin himself. *The Martyrdom of Justin*—a book about him but not from him—relates how that happened:

> [W]icked decrees were passed against the godly Christians in town and country, to force them to offer libations to vain idols; and accordingly the holy men, having been apprehended, were brought before the prefect of Rome, Rusticus by name. And when they had been brought before his judgment-seat, said to Justin, 'Obey the gods at once, and submit to the kings.' Justin said, 'To obey the commandments of our Saviour Jesus Christ is worthy neither of blame nor of condemnation.' Rusticus the prefect said, 'What kind of doctrines do you profess?' Justin said, 'I have endeavoured to learn all doctrines; but I have acquiesced at last in the true doctrines, those namely of the Christians, even though they do not please those who hold false opinions.'[151]

The outcome of this trial was quite predictable—another Christian martyr, who was scourged and beheaded because

---

[150] Ibid. 3.
[151] The Martyrdom of Justin 1.

he confessed Christ and refused to worship the gods:

> *Rusticus the prefect pronounced sentence, saying, 'Let those who have refused to sacrifice to the gods and to yield to the command of the emperor be scourged, and led away to suffer the punishment of decapitation, according to the laws.'*[152]

Justin's martyrdom ended a life of dedication to the cause of Christianity. Not only had he engaged pagan philosophers by debating with them and explaining Christianity, but also had he addressed the emperor himself so he could explain to a fellow philosopher the "real" Christianity, purged of any misinformation. In order to do so, around 140, Justin had moved his base of operations from Ephesus to the Imperial City of Rome, a hotbed of Gnosticism.

Pagans could hardly tell the difference between Christianity and Gnosticism—it seemed all the same to them. They would connect Gnosticism—and therefore also Christianity—with the work of Simon the Magician. At the time when the first persecution (c. 37) of the early Christian community broke out in Jerusalem, Simon was living there. By his magic arts—because of which he was called "Magus"—and by his teachings in which he announced himself as the "great power of God," he had made a name for himself and had won adherents.

Simon the Magician was an old acquaintance of Early Christianity. When the Apostles Peter and John came to Samaria to bestow on the believers the outpouring of the Spirit, which was accompanied by miraculous manifestations, Simon offered them money, desiring them to grant him what he regarded as magical power, so that he also

---

[152] Ibid. 5.

by the laying on of hands could bestow the Holy Ghost, and thereby produce such miraculous results. Full of indignation at such an offer, Peter had rebuked him sharply, exhorted him to penance and conversion and warned him of the wickedness of his conduct.[153] Later, Simon came to Rome during the reign of the Emperor Claudius and by his magic arts won many followers. Irenaeus held him as being one of the founders of Gnosticism and said that it was he who appeared among the Jews as the Son, in Samaria as the Father, and among other nations as the Holy Spirit.

The false identification of Christianity with Gnosticism was one of the reasons why Justin sent his *First Apology* to the Imperial Court. He addressed it to Emperor Antoninus—a discussion from philosopher to philosopher—but with the purpose of assuring the emperor he had nothing to fear from the followers of Jesus Christ:

> [W]e demand that the charges against the Christians be investigated, and that, if these be substantiated, they be punished as they deserve; [or rather, indeed, we ourselves will punish them.] But if no one can convict us of anything, true reason forbids you, for the sake of a wicked rumour, to wrong blameless men, and indeed rather yourselves, who think fit to direct affairs, not by judgment, but by passion.[154]

One of the charges against Christians was that they were atheists—similar to the way Socrates had been declared an atheist. Justin refutes this allegation as follows:

> And we confess that we are atheists, so far as gods of this sort are concerned, but not with respect to the most true God, the Father of

---

[153] Acts 8:9-29.
[154] First Apology 2.

> righteousness and temperance and the other virtues, who is free from all impurity. But both Him, and the Son (who came forth from Him and taught us these things, and the host of the other good angels who follow and are made like to Him), and the prophetic Spirit, we worship and adore, knowing them in reason and truth, and declaring without grudging to every one who wishes to learn, as we have been taught.[155]

Other charges against Christians were based on ignorance about their beliefs, their activities, their rites and practices. So Justin describes to the emperor what Christians really believe and do. He also explains to the emperor how Christian morals differ from pagan morals:

> [W]e who formerly delighted in fornication, but now embrace chastity alone; we who formerly used magical arts, dedicate ourselves to the good and unbegotten God; we who valued above all things the acquisition of wealth and possessions, now bring what we have into a common stock, and communicate to every one in need; we who hated and destroyed one another, and on account of their different manners would not live with men of a different tribe, now, since the coming of Christ, live familiarly with them, and pray for our enemies, and endeavour to persuade those who hate us unjustly to live conformably to the good precepts of Christ, to the end that they may become partakers with us of the same joyful hope of a reward from God the ruler of all.[156]

Justin also tried to debunk the myths about the Eucharist Christians celebrate each Sunday. It gives us a good insight as to how Christians celebrated the Eucharist:

---

[155] Ibid. 6.
[156] First Apology of Justin 14.

> [W]e bless the Maker of all through His Son Jesus Christ, and through the Holy Ghost. And on the day called Sunday, all who live in cities or in the country gather together to one place, and the memoirs of the apostles or the writings of the prophets are read, as long as time permits; then, when the reader has ceased, the president verbally instructs, and exhorts to the imitation of these good things. Then we all rise together and pray, and, as we before said, when our prayer is ended, bread and wine and water are brought, and the president in like manner offers prayers and thanksgivings, according to his ability, and the people assent, saying Amen; and there is a distribution to each, and a participation of that over which thanks have been given, and to those who are absent a portion is sent by the deacons. And they who are well to do, and willing, give what each thinks fit; and what is collected is deposited with the president, who succours the orphans and widows and those who, through sickness or any other cause, are in want, and those who are in bonds and the strangers sojourning among us, and in a word takes care of all who are in need. But Sunday is the day on which we all hold our common assembly, because it is the first day on which God, having wrought a change in the darkness and matter, made the world; and Jesus Christ our Saviour on the same day rose from the dead. For He was crucified on the day before that of Saturn (Saturday); and on the day after that of Saturn, which is the day of the Sun, having appeared to His apostles and disciples, He taught them these things, which we have submitted to you also for your consideration.[157]

What is ultimately at the foundation of Christianity? Justin is

---

[157] Ibid. 67.

coming to the point where all his philosophical groundwork is coming to a head:

> *Our teacher of these things is Jesus Christ, who also was born for this purpose, and was crucified under Pontius Pilate, procurator of Judæa, in the times of Tiberius Cæsar; and that we reasonably worship Him, having learned that He is the Son of the true God Himself, and holding Him in the second place, and the prophetic Spirit in the third.*[158]

Irenaeus of Lyons (130-202)

Originally, Irenaeus came from Asia Minor and had, as a boy, heard Polycarp speak. As a young man, he went to Rome where he became a student of Justin. Ultimately he made his way to the Greek-speaking port city of Lyons, Gaul's thriving trade center in what is now called France. He was on a mission there. Born in Asia, he ended up in Gaul, in present-day France—symbolizing the universality of the Church. It seems that Polycarp himself had started this mission to the "wild west." So Irenaeus had good reason to tell us that he had learned the faith from Polycarp, who in turn had learned from John the Apostle. The link all the way to Jesus was secured.

In 177, Marcus Aurelius' persecution would finally reach Gaul. Soon the Church in Lyons would be decimated by what was probably the worst persecution to hit the Church since Nero's great tribulation at Rome. Once Lyons' bishop Photinus had suffered the same fate as his mentor Polycarp, Irenaeus was ordained as his successor. Beginning shortly after his ordination, Irenaeus set out to compose his monumental work briefly called *Against Heresies*, which he

---

[158] The First Apology 13.

would finish around 188. His original target was a heresy called Valentianism, which is an offshoot of Gnosticism and had also much in common with Docetism. Started in the East, it had now begun to penetrate the newly evangelized West as well.

In this world inundated with heresies, Irenaeus' work was carved out. Irenaeus saw very clearly that each new generation is exposed to new opportunities for Satan and his heretics. He saw new "churches" opening for business every day, preaching a different brand of "truth" from the one next door. So he also knew he had to work on several fronts in his battle against heresies, but his leading front would be Gnosticism with its "secret" knowledge. He spent a great deal of his energy arguing against the esoteric and elitist notions of Gnosticism, carefully clarifying how orthodox Christianity differed from what these Gnostics were selling.

Nowadays, we are still familiar with secret doctrines and rituals in semi-religious circles: Freemasons are known for their secret rituals; Mormons call their secret ceremonies "sacred"; Voodoo cultivates its own secrets; there are numerous secret societies with secret customs and traditions; some are so secret that even their existence is secret. However, secrecy is foreign to Christianity. Jesus sent his followers out to openly preach the Good News to the world. In the words of the parable, "No one who lights a lamp hides it away or places it [under a bushel basket], but on a lampstand so that those who enter might see the light."[159] Christianity is meant for everyone.

One of Irenaeus' arguments against "secret" knowledge was that it is hard to see why Jesus' closest companions would

---

[159] Lk. 11:33.

have withheld their knowledge from other members in the Church:

> *For if the apostles had known hidden mysteries, which they were in the habit of imparting to the perfect apart and privily from the rest, they would have delivered them especially to those to whom they were also committing the Churches themselves. For they were desirous that these men should be very perfect and blameless in all things, whom also they were leaving behind as their successors, delivering up their own place of government to these men; which men, if they discharged their functions honestly, would be a great boon [to the Church], but if they should fall away, the direst calamity.*[160]

Irenaeus points out that "secret" knowledge means that Gnostics can claim whatever they want, without the possibility of any further verification:

> *Such are the variations existing among them with regard to one [passage], holding discordant opinions as to the same Scriptures; and when the same identical passage is read out, they all begin to purse up their eyebrows, and to shake their heads, and they say that they might indeed utter a discourse transcendently lofty, but that all cannot comprehend the greatness of that thought which is implied in it ... Thus do they, as many as they are, all depart [from each other], holding so many opinions as to one thing, and bearing about their clever notions in secret within themselves.*[161]

Claiming private revelations is against what the apostles have handed on to us and taught us. Irenaeus interrogates

---

[160] Against Heresies 3:3:1.
[161] Ibid. 4:35:4.

the Gnostics directly: how could they ever have discovered more than the apostles?

> *[T]hey have apostatized in their opinions from Him who is God, and imagined that they have themselves discovered more than the apostles, by finding out another god; and [maintained] that the apostles preached the Gospel still somewhat under the influence of Jewish opinions, but that they themselves are purer [in doctrine], and more intelligent, than the apostles.*[162]

Irenaeus calls Gnostics conceited and arrogant when they claim that they themselves know more than all other Christians:

> *They proclaim themselves as being perfect, so that no one can be compared to them with respect to the immensity of their knowledge, nor even were you to mention Paul or Peter, or any other of the apostles. They assert that they themselves know more than all others, and that they alone have imbibed the greatness of the knowledge of that power which is unspeakable. They also maintain that they have attained to a height above all power, and that therefore they are free in every respect to act as they please, having no one to fear in anything.*[163]

What we know about Jesus has not come from private revelations or from "improvers of the apostles," as Irenaeus calls them, but only from God's full revelation in Jesus, handed down to us by the apostles:

> *We have learned from none others the plan of our salvation, than from those through whom the*

---

[162] Ibid. 3:12:12.
[163] Ibid. 1:13:6.

> *Gospel has come down to us, which they did at one time proclaim in public, and, at a later period, by the will of God, handed down to us in the Scriptures, to be the ground and pillar of our faith. For it is unlawful to assert that they preached before they possessed perfect knowledge, as some do even venture to say, boasting themselves as improvers of the apostles. For, after our Lord rose from the dead, [the apostles] were invested with power from on high when the Holy Spirit came down [upon them], were filled from all [His gifts], and had perfect knowledge: they departed to the ends of the earth, preaching the glad tidings of the good things [sent] from God to us, and proclaiming the peace of heaven to men, who indeed do all equally and individually possess the Gospel of God.*[164]

There is only one way Christians can learn from God's full revelation in his Son Jesus—follow the chain back to the apostles:

> *The blessed apostles, then, having founded and built up the Church, committed into the hands of Linus the office of the episcopate. Of this Linus, Paul makes mention in the Epistles to Timothy. To him succeeded Anacletus; and after him, in the third place from the apostles, Clement was allotted the bishopric. This man, as he had seen the blessed apostles, and had been conversant with them, might be said to have the preaching of the apostles still echoing [in his ears], and their traditions before his eyes. Nor was he alone [in this], for there were many still remaining who had received instructions from the apostles.*[165]

---

[164] Ibid. 3:1:1.
[165] Ibid. 3:3.

Another front Irenaeus had to defend is the heresy of Docetism, including Valentianism, by insisting that Christ was both the Word made flesh and the Word through whom God created the world:

> *And I have proved already, that it is the same thing to say that He appeared merely to outward seeming, and [to affirm] that He received nothing from Mary. For He would not have been one truly possessing flesh and blood, by which He redeemed us, unless He had summed up in Himself the ancient formation of Adam. Vain therefore are the disciples of Valentinus who put forth this opinion, in order that they may exclude the flesh from salvation, and cast aside what God has fashioned.*[166]

And here is his main argument against Docetism: Jesus could have only redeemed us if he really and truly gave his soul for our souls, and his flesh for our flesh—otherwise our redemption would be null and void:

> *Since the Lord thus has redeemed us through His own blood, giving His soul for our souls, and His flesh for our flesh, and has also poured out the Spirit of the Father for the union and communion of God and man, imparting indeed God to men by means of the Spirit, and, on the other hand, attaching man to God by His own incarnation, and bestowing upon us at His coming immortality durably and truly, by means of communion with God—all the doctrines of the heretics fall to ruin.*[167]

Another front Irenaeus had to defend is the heresy of Ebionism by maintaining that the God of the New Testament

---

[166] Ibid. 5:1:2.
[167] Ibid. 5:1.

could not be separated from the God of the Old Covenant; and that the "spiritual" teaching of the Sermon on the Mount could not be separated from the moral law of Mount Sinai. He defended the Old Testament by describing God's salvation as that of a *pedagogue* who knows how to adjust his teaching to the level of his "students":

> *Thus it was, too, that God formed man at the first, because of His munificence; but chose the patriarchs for the sake of their salvation; and prepared a people beforehand, teaching the headstrong to follow God; and raised up prophets upon earth, accustoming man to bear His Spirit [within him], and to hold communion with God. ... Thus, in a variety of ways, He adjusted the human race to an agreement with salvation. ... Moreover, He instructed the people, who were prone to turn to idols, instructing them by repeated appeals to persevere and to serve God, calling them to the things of primary importance by means of those which were secondary. ... they learned to fear God, and to continue devoted to His service.*[168]

When it comes to the New Testament, Irenaeus identified the four legitimate Gospels that we still acknowledge today:

> *Matthew also issued a written Gospel among the Hebrews in their own dialect, while Peter and Paul were preaching at Rome, and laying the foundations of the Church. After their departure, Mark, the disciple and interpreter of Peter, did also hand down to us in writing what had been preached by Peter. Luke also, the companion of Paul, recorded in a book the Gospel preached by him. Afterwards, John, the disciple of the Lord, who also had leaned upon His breast, did himself*

---

[168] Ibid. 4:14:2-3.

publish a Gospel during his residence at Ephesus in Asia.[169]

After all his attacks on heresies, the question might arise how the Church knows she is dealing with heresies. Irenaeus dares to face this critical question head on. As a matter of fact, what is it that makes the writings of Church Fathers more reliable than the writings of heretics? Gnostics had tried to back their claims by referring to some apostles whose true movements supposedly had been lost to history, or speaking of "later and fuller" revelations passed down by Peter or Paul "in secret." Well, these trials had already been invalidated by Irenaeus in other passages. But for the Church, there had to be a better way to legitimize her teachings. Take this case, says Irenaeus:

> *Suppose there arise a dispute relative to some important question among us, should we not have recourse to the most ancient Churches with which the apostles held constant intercourse, and learn from them what is certain and clear in regard to the present question? For how should it be if the apostles themselves had not left us writings? Would it not be necessary, [in that case,] to follow the course of the tradition which they handed down to those to whom they did commit the Churches?*[170]

"Tradition" is the key-word here, and tradition goes back to Jesus through the chain of apostolic succession. Tradition is that which we find at every place and at every time in all of the Church:

> *For, although the languages of the world are dissimilar, yet the import of the tradition is one*

---

[169] Ibid. 3:1:1.
[170] Ibid. 3:4:1.

> and the same. *For the Churches which have been planted in Germany do not believe or hand down anything different, nor do those in Spain, nor those in Gaul, nor those in the East, nor those in Egypt, nor those in Libya, nor those which have been established in the central regions of the world. But as the sun, that creature of God, is one and the same throughout the whole world, so also the preaching of the truth shines everywhere, and enlightens all men that are willing to come to a knowledge of the truth.*[171]

Irenaeus himself is part of this chain of apostolic succession. He recalls in his five-volume work *Against Heresies* how he studied his theology at the feet of Polycarp, and how Polycarp was personally taught by John the Apostle, who was personally taught by Jesus Christ, who in turn was personally taught by God the Father Almighty. It is the chain of the apostolic succession that keeps the Church together and on the right path.

This does not only apply to Irenaeus himself but to any other bishop in this line of succession. So long as Polycarp, Irenaeus' own father in the Lord, was alive, it was still possible for a Church Father to learn the message of the apostles directly from one of his own personal disciples. But once they are all gone, we depend on their successors:

> *The blessed apostles, then, having founded and built up the Church, committed into the hands of Linus the office of the episcopate. Of this Linus, Paul makes mention in the Epistles to Timothy. To him succeeded Anacletus; and after him, in the third place from the apostles, Clement was allotted the bishopric. This man, as he had seen the blessed apostles, and had been conversant*

---

[171] Ibid. 1:10:2.

> *with them, might be said to have the preaching of the apostles still echoing [in his ears], and their traditions before his eyes. Nor was he alone [in this], for there were many still remaining who had received instructions from the apostles. ... In this order, and by this succession, the ecclesiastical tradition from the apostles, and the preaching of the truth, have come down to us. And this is most abundant proof that there is one and the same vivifying faith, which has been preserved in the Church from the apostles until now, and handed down in truth.*[172]

From this follows that Christians need to hold on to the authority and tradition of those who handed down the truth to them in the line of succession:

> *Wherefore it is incumbent to obey the presbyters who are in the Church—those who, as I have shown, possess the succession from the apostles; those who, together with the succession of the episcopate, have received the certain gift of truth, according to the good pleasure of the Father. But [it is also incumbent] to hold in suspicion others who depart from the primitive succession, and assemble themselves together in any place whatsoever, [looking upon them] either as heretics of perverse minds, or as schismatics puffed up and self-pleasing, or again as hypocrites, acting thus for the sake of lucre and vainglory. For all these have fallen from the truth.*[173]

All those who deviate from Church authority and Church tradition "do not join themselves to the Church, but defraud themselves of life through their perverse opinions and

---

[172] Ibid. 3:3:3.
[173] Ibid. 4:26:2.

infamous behaviour." This verdict against heretics is immediately followed by a key passage: "For where the Church is, there is the Spirit of God; and where the Spirit of God is, there is the Church, and every kind of grace; but the Spirit is truth."[174]

As long as we hold on to the Tradition of the Church, "all the doctrines of the heretics fall to ruin."[175] Yet, Irenaeus foresaw the time that the very idea of one holy, catholic, and apostolic Church might be forgotten by many. We know all too well nowadays how real his fear was and still is. The Church Fathers had reason to be concerned about heretic attacks on the Christian Faith. That threat is still very real in our modern society.

---

[174] Ibid. 3:24:1.
[175] Ibid. 5:1:1.

5. The 4th Generation (180-230)

a. Backdrop

Third-century Rome was a libertarian's paradise, as much so as current societies in the developed world. Citizens of whatever race and creed were free to buy and sell, to propagate ideas, to worship and believe, to choose sexual partners as they pleased. Because there was "freedom of religion" to a certain extent, the empire's polytheism had more to do with a multitude of religions than a multitude of gods.

In this tapestry of religions, Christianity had its own place—perhaps some ten to fifteen percent of the entire population was Christian. Yet, Christianity was still considered a strange cult in the Roman Empire. So it didn't take long for another bloody persecution to take place during the reign of Emperor Septimius Severus (193-211). It was during this persecution, for instance, that Perpetua (22 years old at the time of her death, and mother of an infant she was nursing) and Felicity (a slave imprisoned with her and pregnant at the time) were martyred with other Christians. But in spite of persecution—or probably because of persecution—Christianity was growing. As the Church Father of this generation, Tertullian, would say to his fellow citizens, "The oftener we are mown down by you, the more in number we grow; the blood of

Christians is seed."[176]

At the turn of the century, Alexandria in Egypt began to play an important role in Christianity. It was the city that the Greek conqueror of Egypt, Alexander, some three hundred years before Christ, had named after himself so humbly—Alexandria. Alexander had hoped to unite the world through the spread of Greek culture, and he had been very successful in doing so. From his time forward, the common language and culture of the entire Mediterranean world was Greek. When the Romans took over, they simply coopted the Greek language, the Greek gods, the Greek classics, and Greek philosophy. From then on, Latin was mostly used in the government and the army, while Greek was used in schools and the marketplace. No wonder the inscription of Jesus' cross was written in Aramaic, Latin, and Greek.

During this time, the Church of Alexandria was spared most of the persecutions, but it was menaced by heretical sects of every stripe. Numerous ideas were in the air: ideas of Plato, the Stoics, and the Gnostics. Culture was slowly changing all across the Roman Empire, most notably in its Western part, and so was the knowledge of Greek. Tertullian in Carthage, in present-day Tunisia, would become the first Christian Church Father to write in Latin. Church Fathers of this generation had no longer a direct link with the apostles. Once people like Polycarp and Ignatius had died, all Gospel preaching would have to come "second hand"—from fourth-generation disciples. Nevertheless, new Church Fathers such as Clement of Alexandria and Tertullian of Carthage were ready to take over the torch.

Although the life of Christians was constantly threatened by

---

[176] The Apology 50.

persecutions, the way they lived their lives had not changed much. Here is how Tertullian explains to the Proconsul of Africa the way Christians live their Christian lives:

> *We are a body knit together as such by a common religious profession, by unity of discipline, and by the bond of a common hope. We meet together as an assembly and congregation, that, offering up prayer to God as with united force, we may wrestle with Him in our supplications. This violence God delights in. We pray, too, for the emperors, for their ministers and for all in authority, for the welfare of the world, for the prevalence of peace, for the delay of the final consummation. We assemble to read our sacred writings, if any peculiarity of the times makes either forewarning or reminiscence needful. However it be in that respect, with the sacred words we nourish our faith, we animate our hope, we make our confidence more steadfast; and no less by inculcations of God's precepts we confirm good habits. In the same place also exhortations are made, rebukes and sacred censures are administered.*
>
> *The tried men of our elders preside over us, obtaining that honour not by purchase, but by established character. There is no buying and selling of any sort in the things of God. Though we have our treasure-chest, it is not made up of purchase-money, as of a religion that has its price. On the monthly day, if he likes, each puts in a small donation; but only if it be his pleasure, and only if he be able: for there is no compulsion; all is voluntary. These gifts are, as it were, piety's deposit fund. For they are not taken thence and spent on feasts, and drinking-bouts, and eating-houses, but to support and bury poor people, to supply the wants of boys and girls destitute of*

means and parents, and of old persons confined now to the house; such, too, as have suffered shipwreck; and if there happen to be any in the mines, or banished to the islands, or shut up in the prisons, for nothing but their fidelity to the cause of God's Church, they become the nurslings of their confession.[177]

b. Trouble Within: Montanism

During the late 2nd century, Montanus and two women in his company, Prisca and Maximilla, proclaimed themselves as prophets. Their oracles, spoken in ecstasy and "in tongues," were taken as coming verbatim from the Holy Spirit; they basically took over from Jesus just as Jesus had taken over from Moses. In other words, God's revelation was not finished with Jesus, as more prophets would follow and additional revelations would be coming from prophets speaking in ecstasy.

This was the beginning of a new movement, the Montanist movement—basically a pseudo-charismatic movement associated with ecstasy and speaking in tongues. Montanus himself compared a man in ecstasy with a musical instrument, on which the Holy Spirit plays his melodies. It was through ecstasy that Montanists received new "revelations" and new "knowledge" about God and Christianity. Montanus testified that he had experienced an ecstatic visitation of the Paraclete (the Holy Spirit), who gave him the ability to deliver prophetic messages from God. So we could call it Gnosticism in a new disguise—new "knowledge" coming from the Holy Spirit, this time. In orthodox Christianity, the Holy Spirit helps us to better interpret and better understand what was already revealed to us through Jesus Christ, without giving us "new" revelations,

---

[177] Apology 39.

but Montanism was about *new* revelations.

The Church historian Eusebius tells us how it had all started:

> *There is said to be a certain village called Ardabau in that part of Mysia, which borders upon Phrygia. There first, they say, when Gratus was proconsul of Asia, a recent convert, Montanus by name, through his unquenchable desire for leadership, gave the adversary opportunity against him. And he became beside himself, and being suddenly in a sort of frenzy and ecstasy, he raved, and began to babble and utter strange things, prophesying in a manner contrary to the constant custom of the Church handed down by tradition from the beginning.*[178]

The heresy of Montanism was spreading like wild fire according to Eusebius:

> *The followers of Montanus, Alcibiades and Theodotus in Phrygia were now first giving wide circulation to their assumption in regard to prophecy—for the many other miracles that, through the gift of God, were still wrought in the different churches caused their prophesying to be readily credited by many.*[179]

What we have here is the "Church of the Spirit" plotted against the "Church of bishops." Montanism was in essence an anti-hierarchical movement. Presumably, the Paraclete, or Holy Spirit, had come to purify the Church—similar to what Pentecostals might say today. Montanus declared: "I am the Father, the Word, and the Paraclete." He was ultimately out to challenge the teaching authority of the Church and her bishops. Montanism was presented as a

---

[178] Church History 5:16:7.
[179] Ibid. 5:3.

"New Prophecy."

But there was also another side to Montanism: its rigorism. Montanists were rigorists, advocating the harshest possible moral standards for the Church and her members. Their leaders channeled revelations from the Holy Spirit urging moral rigor, especially chastity, fasting, and willingness to face martyrdom rather than flee or pay bribes. Remarriage after the death of a spouse was strictly forbidden, and there is some indication that serious sins—such as murder, honoring Roman deities, adultery, and refusing to confess one's Christianity—may have been considered unforgivable once a believer had been baptized. In line with this, Montanists judged bishops as disqualified if they did not meet a "pure" standard of Christian life. Thus this heresy had fallen from evangelical freedom into Jewish legalism. Later we will see similar trends in another heresy, Donatism (see 9.b).

As to be expected, a heresy like this opens the gate for any heretic to become a legitimized prophet based on private revelations. No wonder, Montanists were soon assembling together into their own "pure" congregations, making for a heresy that led to a schism or a cult. They called themselves "spiritual Christians," to distinguish and separate themselves from "carnal Christians." More recently we have seen something similar with movements that started with Joseph Smith, founder of the Latter Day Saints (Mormons), or with Charles Russell, founder of the Jehovah's Witnesses. They founded cults that had their own private revelations too and used them to start a new church.

c. Defenders of the Faith

Clement of Alexandria (150-215)

After the persecution that broke out in Athens under Emperor Severus in 202, Clement left for Alexandria where he spent most of his remaining years. When he arrived in Alexandria, it was the largest and most vibrant city in the world, second only to Rome. He served as the head of Alexandria's catechetical school there. One of his students was the 5th generation Church Father Origen (see 6.c). Entrusted to evangelizing and training, Clement was convinced that rejecting philosophy and learning would be disastrous for his school and for Christianity. Like Justin, he realized that knowledge of philosophy and literature is an important tool for defending the Christian Faith. The most important point he contributed was his idea regarding the interrelation between Christianity and philosophy: Truth is one and comes from God.

Whereas his contemporary Tertullian would claim that "knowledge" has nothing to do with Faith, Clement would stress that "knowledge" could actually prepare the mind well for the Faith of God's revelation. Faith in the Incarnation, for instance, would greatly benefit if we use the right philosophical concepts, so Clement said. But he is certainly not referring to the kind of "knowledge" Gnostics talk about.

Clement contrasts the true knowledge of the Christian with the false "knowledge" of Gnosticism and Montanism. He applies the same word as Gnostics had used—*gnosis*—but uses it in its original sense—real knowledge—that is, knowledge of truth, not esoteric knowledge. So he is basically taking the Gnostic sting out of knowledge. He calls Christians the "real Gnostics." Whereas Gnosticism had hijacked and corrupted the word "gnosis," Clement is claiming it back: the real "gnosis" is faith in the true God and his only Son Jesus Christ. In his own words, "Well, then, if the Lord is the truth, and wisdom, and power of God, as in truth He is, it is shown that the real Gnostic is he that knows Him, and His Father by Him."[180]

Thus Clement makes quite an effort to explain who the "true Gnostic" is in Christianity. Whereas "gnosis" of Gnostics is some esoteric kind of knowledge, the real knowledge comes from Jesus Christ. The difference between these two is striking. He describes the true Gnostic as follows:

> *He is the Gnostic, who is after the image and likeness of God, who imitates God as far as possible, deficient in none of the things which contribute to the likeness as far as compatible, practising self-restraint and endurance, living righteously, reigning over the passions, bestowing of what he has as far as possible, and doing good both by word and deed.*[181]

Of course, this is much more than a semantic issue. The real "knowledge" is what has been prophesized to us when God revealed himself to us: "Again, prophecy is foreknowledge; and knowledge the understanding of prophecy; being the knowledge of those things known before by the Lord who reveals all things."[182]

Apparently, in Clement's view, faith and knowledge are not each other's opposites. Faith is a form of knowledge, and knowledge is always a form of faith. You cannot believe what you don't know; and you cannot know what you don't believe. A person must *believe* something in order to *know*

---

[180] Stromata 2:11.
[181] Ibid. 2:19.
[182] Ibid. 2:12.

it:

> *[I]n order to believe truly in the Son, we must* believe *that He is the Son, and that He came, and how, and for what, and respecting His passion; and we must* know *who is the Son of God. Now neither is knowledge without faith, nor faith without knowledge. Nor is the Father without the Son; for the Son is with the Father. And the Son is the true teacher respecting the Father; and that we may* believe *in the Son, we must* know *the Father, with whom also is the Son. Again, in order that we may* know *the Father, we must* believe *in the Son, that it is the Son of God who teaches; for from faith to knowledge by the Son is the Father. And the knowledge of the Son and Father, which is according to the gnostic rule— that which in reality is gnostic— is the attainment and comprehension of the truth by the truth.*[183]

In other words, there is no faith without knowledge. We cannot claim we have faith if we don't have some kind of knowledge. This requires also something like learning and training:

> *But as we say that a man can be a believer without learning, so also we assert that it is impossible for a man without* learning *to comprehend the things which are declared in the faith. But to adopt what is well said, and not to adopt the reverse, is caused not simply by faith, but by faith combined with knowledge. But if ignorance is want of training and of instruction, then teaching produces knowledge of divine and human things.*[184]

---

[183] Ibid. 5:1.
[184] Ibid. 1:6.

The knowledge of the Greeks—of the Greek philosophers, that is—is in fact also knowledge, but of an imperfect and incomplete nature; it is a dim kind of knowledge of God: "the philosophers among the Greeks, who from the Hebrew prophets before the coming of the Lord received fragments of the truth, not with full knowledge."[185] And also, "the excellent among the Greeks worshipped the same God as we, but that they had not learned by perfect knowledge that which was delivered by the Son."[186] In other words, "man is made principally for the knowledge of God."[187] That's how Clement, like Justin, remained in dialogue with the pagan philosophers, trying to help them search for the full truth that he himself had found in Christianity.

Clement was realistic enough to know that philosophy was seen as a threat to the Faith in the eyes of many Christians. So he pleaded to them not to close their eyes for the potential philosophy had to strengthen their Faith. He uses the analogy of Ulysses and the Sirens:

> *But the multitude are frightened at the Hellenic philosophy, as children are at masks, being afraid lest it lead them astray. ... But, as seems, the most of those who are inscribed with the Name, like the companions of Ulysses, handle the word unskilfully, passing by not the Sirens, but the rhythm and the melody, stopping their ears with ignorance; since they know that, after lending their ears to Hellenic studies, they will never subsequently be able to retrace their steps. But he who culls what is useful for the advantage of the catechumens ... must not abstain from erudition, like irrational animals; but he must*

---

[185] Ibid. 1:17.
[186] Ibid. 6:5.
[187] Ibid. 6:8.

> *collect as many aids as possible for his hearers. But he must by no means linger over these studies, except solely for the advantage accruing from them; so that, on grasping and obtaining this, he may be able to take his departure home to the true philosophy, which is a strong cable for the soul, providing security from everything.*[188]

With his philosophy, Clement of Alexandria successfully battled the "false knowledge" of Gnosticism. But he was also someone who opposed the heresy of Montanism very vehemently. He fulminates against false prophets, including the "prophets" Montanism had produced. He explains what the danger is of speaking in tongues and of having prophecies through ecstasy. He warns us that somehow they may easily open the door for demonic voices if not tested carefully:

> *The devil is called thief and robber; having mixed false prophets with the prophets, as tares with the wheat. All, then, that came before the Lord, were thieves and robbers; not absolutely all men, but all the false prophets, and all who were not properly sent by Him. For the false prophets possessed the prophetic name dishonestly, being prophets, but prophets of the liar For the Lord says, You are of your father the devil; and the lusts of your father you will do. He was a murderer from the beginning, and abode not in the truth, because there is no truth in him.*
>
> *But among the lies, the false prophets also told some true things. And in reality they prophesied in an ecstasy, as the servants of the apostate. And the Shepherd, the angel of repentance, says to Hermas*[189], *of the false prophet: For he speaks*

---

[188] Ibid. 6:10-11.
[189] The Book *Shepherd of Hermas* (early 2nd century) was

> *some truths. For the devil fills him with his own spirit, if perchance he may be able to cast down any one from what is right.*[190]

Clement's remarks do not deny, of course, that speaking in tongues may be a valuable charism in the Catholic Church, for the Apostle Paul speaks about it—on condition it's done with love.[191] As the Catechism puts it, "Charisms are to be accepted with gratitude by the person who receives them and by all members of the Church as well. They are a wonderfully rich grace for the apostolic vitality and for the holiness of the entire Body of Christ, provided they really are genuine gifts of the Holy Spirit and are used in full conformity with authentic promptings of this same Spirit."[192] That's where Clement's warning becomes pivotal: they may lead us astray if not tested carefully.

Somewhere else Clement mentions a somewhat cryptic link between ecstasies and demons. He warns us that those who speak in ecstasies think they know their Master's Voice, but their master may not be God but Satan, whose language, or "dialect," they speak. A human being can be "under the influence" of evil forces, following "orders" that do not come from God. When Montanists in their ecstasies speak against their bishop, for instance, they do not use the Voice of God. Clement compares this with what Plato had said earlier:

> *".Plato attributes a dialect also to the gods, forming this conjecture mainly from dreams and oracles, and especially from demoniacs, who do not speak their own language or dialect, but that*

---

considered canonical by Irenaeus, but never made it to the final canon.

[190] Stromata 1: 17.
[191] 1 Cor. 13:1-2.
[192] Catechism of the Catholic Church 800.

> *of the demons who have taken possession of them.*[193]

How should we assess Clement of Alexandria? He is hard to judge, given the fact that his writing is not very precise and orderly. Yet, he was exceptionally well-read and had a thorough knowledge of the whole range of Biblical and Christian literature. It was his main intent, with philosophy as an instrument, to transform Faith into knowledge. The Gnostics had pretended to do the same, but they had come up with an exotic, esoteric kind of knowledge. The Montanists had tried something similar, but their knowledge was fake knowledge based on spurious revelations shown in ecstasies. Clement, instead, presented a "solid" faith based on Scripture and Tradition.

Tertullian of Carthage (160-220)

First it needs to be stated that Tertullian did not attack Montanism like Clement did, but actually joined the Montanists later in life. Although started in Turkey, the Montanists would meet with much more sympathy in North Africa. Their greatest conquest was the gifted and fiery, but eccentric and rigoristic Tertullian. He became, in the year 201 or 202, a most energetic and influential advocate of Montanism, without, however, formally seceding from the Catholic Church, whose doctrines he continued to defend against the heretics.

Church Father Augustine relates, later on, that Tertullian left the Montanists, and founded a new sect, which was called after him, but was, through Augustine's help, reconciled to the Catholic congregation of Carthage. The following of Tertullian cannot have been large; yet a Tertullianist sect did

---

[193] Stromata 1: 21.

survive him, but its remnants were reconciled to the Church. Later on, Origen was uncertain whether they were schismatics or heretics. At all events, Tertullian was not excommunicated, and his orthodox writings were always highly esteemed.

Tertullian was first of all a theologian, but always in his role as a lawyer. He always wrote with an adversary in mind, always keen to win a case. One of his "cases" was *freedom of religion*, which he defended forcefully against the idea of religion imposed by the government. In a 212 letter to Scapula, the proconsul of Africa, he wrote:

> *We are worshippers of one God, of whose existence and character Nature teaches all men; at whose lightnings and thunders you tremble, whose benefits minister to your happiness. You think that others, too, are gods, whom we know to be devils. However, it is a fundamental human right, a privilege of nature, that every man should worship according to his own convictions: one man's religion neither harms nor helps another man. It is assuredly no part of religion to compel religion— to which free-will and not force should lead us— the sacrificial victims even being required of a willing mind.*[194]

Not surprisingly, as a former lawyer, Tertullian was a fierce fighter against heresies. He accuses heretics of "removing landmarks," but they have no right to do so on *his* property, for he considers "Church property" his own "property":

> *For as they are heretics, they cannot be true Christians, because it is not from Christ that they get that which they pursue of their own mere choice, and from the pursuit incur and admit the*

---

[194] Letter to Scapula 2.

> name of heretics. Thus, not being Christians, they have acquired no right to the Christian Scriptures; and it may be very fairly said to them, Who are you? When and whence did you come? As you are none of mine, what have you to do with that which is mine? Indeed, Marcion, by what right do you hew my wood? By whose permission, Valentinus, are you diverting the streams of my fountain? By what power, Apelles, are you removing my landmarks? This is my property.[195]

Tertullian explains the nature of the Church in his *Prescription Against Heretics*, which deals with the nature of truth. The Church, he says, has always made use of the Scriptures and is the only one who may rightly use them and interpret them. Heretics are excluded from every discussion, and only the orthodox and Apostolic Church has the right to determine what qualifies as Christian doctrine and what does not.

Unlike Clement of Alexandria and unlike Justin before him, Tertullian showed no interest in accommodating Christian doctrine to pagan philosophy. He rather accepted and even glorified seeming philosophical or logical contradictions—contradictions such as "God is three and yet one," or "Jesus is man and yet God." His famous saying was, "What indeed has Athens [the city of philosophers] to do with Jerusalem [the city of believers]? What concord is there between the Academy and the Church?"[196] Somewhere else he says about Christian doctrine, "it is by all means to be believed, because it is absurd."[197] The word "absurd" is probably a poor translation; he actually spoke of "inapt" [*ineptum*], which

---

[195] Prescription Against Heretics 37.
[196] Ibid. 7.
[197] On the Flesh of Christ 5.

could be translated as "improper" or so.

There remains a haunting question: If Tertullian is considered such a champion of orthodoxy, such a fierce fighter against heresies, and such a strong defender of the Church, how could he join Montanism and become a heretic himself? Why was Tertullian never condemned by the Church? The main reason is that he contributed immensely to the theology of the *Trinity*. He accomplished this by writing against the heresy of Praxeas—an early form of Modalism that we will encounter later again (see 7.b). Praxeas believed in the unity of the Godhead and vehemently disagreed with any attempt to divide the personalities of the Father, Son, and Holy Spirit. By this one-sided focus on the unity of the Godhead, he made Father and Son and Holy Spirit identical to each other. Tertullian describes the problems of this heresy as follows:

> *In various ways has the devil rivalled and resisted the truth. Sometimes his aim has been to destroy the truth by defending it. He maintains that there is one only Lord, the Almighty Creator of the world, in order that out of this doctrine of the unity he may fabricate a heresy. He says that the Father Himself came down into the Virgin, was Himself born of her, Himself suffered, indeed was Himself Jesus Christ.*[198]

Tertullian explained extensively what is wrong with Praxeas' heresy. Praxeas falsely believes, according to Tertullian,

> *that one cannot believe in One Only God in any other way than by saying that the Father, the Son, and the Holy Ghost are the very selfsame Person. As if in this way also one were not All, in that All are of One, by unity (that is) of*

---

[198] Against Praxeas 1.

> *substance; while the mystery of the dispensation is still guarded, which distributes the Unity into a Trinity, placing in their order the three Persons— the Father, the Son, and the Holy Ghost: three, however, not in condition, but in degree; not in substance, but in form; not in power, but in aspect; yet of one substance, and of one condition, and of one power, inasmuch as He is one God, from whom these degrees and forms and aspects are reckoned, under the name of the Father, and of the Son, and of the Holy Ghost.*[199]

From this, Tertullian concludes the following:

> *Away, then, with those 'Antichrists who deny the Father and the Son.' For they deny the Father, when they say that He is the same as the Son; and they deny the Son, when they suppose Him to be the same as the Father, by assigning to Them things which are not Theirs, and taking away from Them things which are Theirs.*[200]

In correcting this heresy, Tertullian became the most influential theologian the Church ever had. He gave us this outline of a *Trinitarian* theology:

> *[T]here is one only God, but under the following dispensation, or οἰκονομία [economy] as it is called, that this one only God has also a Son, His Word, who proceeded from Himself, by whom all things were made, and without whom nothing was made. Him we believe to have been sent by the Father into the Virgin, and to have been born of her— being both Man and God, the Son of Man and the Son of God, and to have been called by the name of Jesus Christ; we believe Him to have suffered, died, and been buried, according to the*

---

[199] Ibid. 2.
[200] Ibid. 31.

> *Scriptures, and, after He had been raised again by the Father and taken back to heaven, to be sitting at the right hand of the Father, and that He will come to judge the quick and the dead; who sent also from heaven from the Father, according to His own promise, the Holy Ghost, the Paraclete, the sanctifier of the faith of those who believe in the Father, and in the Son, and in the Holy Ghost.*[201]

His writing *Against Praxeas* was significant because in it he uses general phrases and terminology that would be used centuries later in Christology and Trinitarianism. One significant aspect of Tertullian's Trinitarian doctrine is his insistence on the divine economy [*oeconomia*]: God is one, but the divine persons are associated with each other based on their economy, or work. Just as there are in God three persons and only one substance, in Jesus Christ there are two substances (divinity and humanity) both of which belong to a single person.

Tertullian coined some very orthodox ideas surrounding these truths—even in spite of his lapse into Montanism. But he also realized, his Trinitarian theology would raise some eyebrows:

> *If the number of the Trinity also offends you, as if it were not connected in the simple Unity, I ask you how it is possible for a Being who is merely and absolutely One and Singular, to speak in plural phrase, saying, Let us make man in our own image, and after our own likeness? ... it was because He had already His Son close at His side, as a second Person, His own Word, and a third Person also, the Spirit in the Word, that He purposely adopted the plural phrase, 'Let us*

---

[201] Ibid. 2.

> *make'; and, 'in our image'; and, 'become as one of us'.*[202]

When it comes to the explanation of how the human and the divine are related in Jesus Christ, Tertullian made another brilliant and decisive contribution. He taught us that in Christ, there is one person with two natures [*substantiae*], human and divine. Thus he prepared the way for other Church Fathers to follow:

> *Neither the flesh becomes Spirit, nor the Spirit flesh. In one Person they no doubt are well able to be co-existent. Of them Jesus consists—Man, of the flesh; of the Spirit, God—and the angel designated Him as 'the Son of God,' in respect of that nature, in which He was Spirit, reserving for the flesh the appellation 'Son of Man.'*[203]

It is important to notice that it was Tertullian who first used the word "Trinity" [*Trinitas*] to describe God. Does this mean he invented not only a new word but also a new concept? Certainly not. The idea was old, only the word was new. Think of "gravity." Did the ancient Romans know about gravity? Of course they did, for they saw it all around them. But the technical term in itself came much later to designate and explain a force between objects, a force that falling apples and orbiting planets have in common. Talking "Trinity" to first-century Christians would have been like talking "general relativity" to Isaac Newton.

So, were Peter and Paul "Trinitarians"? Did the first Christians know about the Trinity? They knew about the concept but did not know the word yet, for the introduction of that term had to wait for Tertullian. But they certainly

---

[202] Ibid. 12; italics added.
[203] Ibid. 27.

knew that which the word would later refer to. Somehow the apostles knew already that God is a Trinitarian God—one God in three Persons. They baptized new Christians in the Name of the Father, the Son, and the Holy Spirit. Paul could not have expressed it more clearly: "The grace of the Lord Jesus Christ and the love of God and the fellowship of the holy Spirit be with all of you."[204] We find Trinitarian terminology all over the New Testament—e.g. Mt. 28:19 and 2 Cor. 13: 14 and Hebr. 9:14.

Trinitarian terminology was quite common, not only in the New Testament but also among the early Church Fathers. Clement of Rome had already used Trinitarian terminology as early as the 90s: "For, as God lives, and as the Lord Jesus Christ and the Holy Ghost live."[205] And so had Irenaeus: "The Church, though dispersed through our the whole world, even to the ends of the earth, has received from the apostles and their disciples this faith: [She believes] in one God, the Father Almighty, Maker of heaven, and earth, and the sea, and all things that are in them; and in one Christ Jesus, the Son of God, who became incarnate for our salvation; and in the Holy Spirit."[206] And now it was Tertullian who would give it a thorough theological basis, ready to be worked with by the next generation of Church Fathers. No wonder, he received a special place in the "Hall of Fame" of the Church Fathers.

---

[204] 2 Cor. 13:14.
[205] First Epistle 58.
[206] Against Heresies 1:10.

6. The 5th Generation (230-280)

a. Backdrop

On January 250, Emperor Decius (201-251) issued one of the most astonishing, yet detrimental, Roman imperial edicts. All the inhabitants of the empire were required to sacrifice by a certain day before the magistrates of their community "for the safety of the empire". When they sacrificed they would obtain a certificate recording the fact that they had complied with the order. That is, the certificate would testify the bearer's loyalty to the ancestral gods and to the consumption of sacrificial food and drink; the certificate also held the names of the officials who had been overseeing the sacrifice.

The goal was to swiftly decapitate the Church by first going after her leadership. Needless to say that this took a heavy toll on the Church everywhere: in Rome, Pope Fabian (236-250) was martyred; in Alexandria, Origen was sent into prison; in Carthage, Cyprian had to flee and hide. However, the very emperor who had drawn the sword against the Christians fell by the sword himself. Origen was released and Cyprian returned home.

Though this persecution had only lasted fourteen months, much damage was done. Many had died for Christ, but also many had compromised by performing the pagan sacrifices or by purchasing fraudulent certificates. Those Christians who had caved in to Roman pressure and agreed to renounce their Faith and offer sacrifice to the gods were termed *lapsi*, "the lapsed." So the question became whether the lapsed should be accepted back in the community, when the storm was over.

This discussion had also reached Rome. After Pope Fabian had been martyred, he was succeeded by Pope Cornelius who was willing to grant absolution to some of the lapsed. Novatian, a scholar and priest in Rome, protested that the new pope had polluted the holiness of the Church by welcoming apostates. Novatian found some bishops who were willing to consecrate him as the lawful bishop of the only legitimate Church in Rome—an anti-pope. When the Church Father Cyprian of Carthage investigated the two elections, he determined that Cornelius, not Novatian, was the legitimate pope. He declared this schism a much greater threat to the Church than any persecution had ever been.

But persecutions were not over yet. After the bloody persecution by Emperor Decius (250-251), another emperor, Valerian (253-260), reached new heights of ruthlessness in his war against Christians. But at the same time, another calamity was emerging: a new kind of "martyrdom" in the form of the plague. The Church historian Eusebius gives us a description of how Christians treated each other during these times of trouble—especially during the spread of the plague or pestilence:

> *The most of our brethren were unsparing in their exceeding love and brotherly kindness. They held fast to each other and visited the sick fearlessly, and ministered to them continually, serving them in Christ. And they died with them most joyfully, taking the affliction of others, and drawing the sickness from their neighbors to themselves and*

> *willingly receiving their pains. And many who cared for the sick and gave strength to others died themselves having transferred to themselves their death.*[207]
>
> *Truly the best of our brethren departed from life in this manner, including some presbyters and deacons and those of the people who had the highest reputation; so that this form of death, through the great piety and strong faith it exhibited, seemed to lack nothing of martyrdom.*[208]
>
> *And they took the bodies of the saints in their open hands and in their bosoms, and closed their eyes and their mouths; and they bore them away on their shoulders and laid them out; and they clung to them and embraced them; and they prepared them suitably with washings and garments. And after a little they received like treatment themselves, for the survivors were continually following those who had gone before them.*[209]

Then Eusebius tells us how different the actions of Christians were compared to the actions of others around them:

> *But with the heathen everything was quite otherwise. They deserted those who began to be sick, and fled from their dearest friends. And they cast them out into the streets when they were half dead, and left the dead like refuse, unburied. They shunned any participation or fellowship with death; which yet, with all their precautions, it was not easy for them to escape.*[210]

---

[207] Church History 7:22:7.
[208] Eusebius 7:22:8.
[209] Church History 7:22:9.
[210] Ibid. 7:22:10.

It is during the turbulence this generation experienced that two new heresies emerged and at least two new Church Fathers appeared on the scene.

b. Trouble Within: Adoptionism | Novatianism

The Church kept battling heresies on several fronts—not only old ones but also new emerging ones. Two in particular would face the Church Fathers of this 5th generation: Adoptionism and Novatianism.

After Tertullian had made clear that Praxeas' one-sided focus on the unity of the Godhead would make Father and Son and Holy Spirit become identical to each other, a new heresy went in the opposite direction by opting for the other extreme: separating Jesus from God, and denying Jesus' divinity. This heresy is commonly called *Adoptionism* (but there are many versions of it).

Adoptionism claims that Jesus himself was not God but was adopted by God. Although he is the Son of God, he is an adoptive son. He was truly man, but not truly God. Thus it denies the eternal pre-existence of Christ. Jesus may be divine from the moment of his adoption, but he is not equal to the Father. This heresy was preached first by Theodotus, "the leather-seller" of Byzantium, but the idea behind it is probably much older. Theodotus taught that Jesus was a man born of a virgin, according to the Council of Jerusalem, that he lived like other men, and was most pious; but that at his baptism in the Jordan, the "Christ" came down upon the man Jesus in the likeness of a dove. Adoptionism is the belief that Jesus was not divine at birth, but was so virtuous that he was adopted later as "Son of God" by the descent of the Spirit on him.

The First Christians: Keeping the Faith in Times of Trouble

Adoptionism is one of two main forms of so-called Monarchianism—the other one is Modalism, which we will discuss later (see 7.b) as a heresy that regards "Father" and "Son" as two different roles of a single divine Person. Adoptionism (also known as dynamic Monarchianism)—although it explicitly affirms Jesus' deity subsequent to events in his life—is a heresy because it implicitly denies his divinity by denying the constant "union in one person" of the eternal Logos to the human nature of Jesus.

Here we have the first new heresy the Church Fathers of this generation had to deal with. The other one was a new, modified version of Montanism. It was a heresy that began with Novatian (200-258), someone we met earlier (see 6.a): an anti-pope who followed Pope Fabian in 251, in opposition to Cornelius, the lawful Bishop of Rome. The schismatic church that he started adopted a new heresy. It claimed that people in grave sin—including those Christians who during the persecution of Emperor Decius had offered to the gods—were permanently excluded from the Church and should be refused absolution. Novatian held that their idolatry was an unpardonable sin, and that the Church had no right to restore to communion anyone who had fallen into it—the so-called "lapsi" whom he considered apostates.

The followers of Novatian named themselves "Puritans" [*katharoi*]. Novatian had refused absolution to idolaters; but his followers went even further and extended this doctrine to include all "mortal sins"—not only idolatry, but also murder, infidelity, and fornication. Most of them even forbade a second marriage, after the death of a spouse. They always had a successor of Novatian at Rome, and almost everywhere they had bishops who governed them. The main works written against them are those of the 5th generation Church Father Cyprian of Carthage. Rome considered Novatian's followers to be heretics for denying that the Church has the power to grant absolution, especially in very serious cases. They certainly curtailed God's mercy. The heresy would later come back in the form of Donatism (see 9.b).

c. Defenders of the Faith

Origen (184-253)

At age eighteen, Origen was appointed rector of the school of Alexandria to become Clement's successor. One of his students pledged to fund seven stenographers to serve Origen, along with seven copyists. Thanks to these helpers, Origen was able to produce more than six thousand books, according to some sources. Especially in his book *De Principiis* (On First Principles), he gave us a systematic exposition of all Christian doctrine.

We have to keep in mind that what is orthodox in one age may be considered heterodox or even heretical in a later one. Sometimes Origen veered off the road, because the road had not been fully marked out yet by the Church. As a result, many of his writings were later destructed as heretic and have most likely been lost forever. Unlike most other Church Fathers, he was never canonized as a saint in the Catholic Church because of some of his teachings. But on many other issues, he was one of the Church Fathers to map out the path for future generations, and to level the road by lowering the mountains and raising the valleys. He hardly ever alludes to himself in his own works; but Eusebius has devoted to him almost the entire sixth book of his "Church History."

Origen was very successful to do all of this during most of his life, but like so many other Church Fathers he was eventually taken prisoner during the persecution of Emperor Decius and died in 253 as a martyr.

The First Christians: Keeping the Faith in Times of Trouble

One of his greatest achievements was explaining the Trinitarian doctrine of the Catholic Church very faithfully and systematically, and giving also very much attention to the nature and role of the Holy Spirit:

> *The particular points clearly delivered in the teaching of the apostles are as follow: First, That there is one God, who created and arranged all things, and who, when nothing existed, called all things into being—God from the first creation and foundation of the world. ... Secondly, That Jesus Christ Himself, who came (into the world), was born of the Father before all creatures; that, after He had been the servant of the Father in the creation of all things—For by Him were all things made—He in the last times, divesting Himself (of His glory), became a man, and was incarnate although God, and while made a man remained the God which He was; that He assumed a body like to our own, differing in this respect only, that it was born of a virgin and of the Holy Spirit: that this Jesus Christ was truly born, and did truly suffer, and did not endure this death common (to man) in appearance only, but did truly die; that He did truly rise from the dead; and that after His resurrection He conversed with His disciples, and was taken up (into heaven). Thirdly, the apostles related that the Holy Spirit was associated in honour and dignity with the Father and the Son.*[211]

As a dedicated Trinitarian, Origen speaks very specifically and unambiguously of the *"unbegotten"* God and the *"only-begotten"* Son—terms that would become even more important for generations to come:

> *In the Acts of the Apostles, the Holy Spirit was*

---

[211] De Principiis, Preface 4.

> *given by the imposition of the apostles' hands in baptism. From all which we learn that the person of the Holy Spirit was of such authority and dignity, that saving baptism was not complete except by the authority of the most excellent Trinity of them all, i.e., by the naming of Father, Son, and Holy Spirit, and by joining to the unbegotten God the Father, and to His only-begotten Son, the name also of the Holy Spirit.*[212]

As to be expected, Origen's theology led to a vehement rejection of Adoptionism. The Church historian Eusebius mentions how Origen immediately could smell trouble when he was told about Beryllus who held views similar to Adoptionism by not accepting the pre-existence and independent divinity of Christ:

> *Beryllus, whom we mentioned recently as bishop of Bostra in Arabia, turned aside from the ecclesiastical standard and attempted to introduce ideas foreign to the faith. He dared to assert that our Saviour and Lord did not pre-exist in a distinct form of being of his own before his abode among men, and that he does not possess a divinity of his own, but only that of the Father dwelling in him.*[213]

Eusebius also mentions how Origen worked hard to bring Beryllus back to the orthodox faith. Through his reasoning skills and friendly moderation, Origen was able to convince Beryllus that he should change his mind about Christ and recognize his divinity at a synod of bishops:

> *Many bishops carried on investigations and discussions with him [Beryllus] on this matter, and Origen having been invited with the others,*

---

[212] Ibid. 1:3:2.
[213] Eusebius 6:33:1.

> *went down at first for a conference with him to ascertain his real opinion. But when he understood his views, and perceived that they were erroneous, having persuaded him by argument, and convinced him by demonstration, he brought him back to the true doctrine, and restored him to his former sound opinion.*[214]

Because the heresy of Adoptionism teaches that Jesus as the Son of God did not have a beginning, Origen went head on to attack such an erroneous view by analyzing what "beginning" means:

> *The beginning and the end is a phrase we usually apply to a thing that is a completed unity; the beginning of a house is its foundation and the end the parapet. We cannot but think of this figure, since Christ is the stone which is the head of the corner, to the great unity of the body of the saved. For Christ the only-begotten Son is all and in all, He is as the beginning in the man He assumed, He is present as the end in the last of the saints, and He is also in those between, or else He is present as the beginning in Adam, as the end in His life on earth.*[215]

Finally, Origen makes a connection between "beginning" and "wisdom":

> *We must observe, then, that the Logos is in the beginning, that is, in wisdom, always. Its being in wisdom, which is called the beginning, does not prevent it from being with God and from being God, and it is not simply with God, but is in the beginning, in wisdom, with God. For he [John] goes on: He was in the beginning with God. He might have said, He was with God; but*

---

[214] Ibid. 6:33:2.
[215] On John 1:34.

> *as He was in the beginning, so He was with God in the beginning, and All things were made by Him, being in the beginning, for God made all things.*[216]

Not surprisingly, Origen's name was so highly esteemed that when there was a question of putting an end to a schism or rooting out a heresy, appeal was made to him. Many subsequent Church Fathers would speak highly of him. However, amidst these expressions of admiration and praise, a few discordant voices were heard. But it cannot be denied that his chief adversaries were always heretics of all colors—Sabellians, Arians, Pelagians, Nestorians, Apollinarists.

What was behind Origen's lifelong warfare against heresies? According to Origen, we have only two lights to guide us here below: Christ and the Church. It is the Church that reflects faithfully the light received from Christ, as the moon reflects the rays of the sun. The distinctive mark of the Catholic is to belong to the Church, to depend on the Church—whereas those who leave the Church walk in darkness and become heretics.

What was the tool for Origen to determine what is orthodox and what is heterodox? It is through the principle of authority that Origen is able to unmask and combat doctrinal errors. He laid down a principle that appeals to the practice of the Church founded on apostolic and ecclesiastical *Tradition*:

> *[S]eeing there are many who think they hold the opinions of Christ, and yet some of these think differently from their predecessors, yet as the teaching of the Church, transmitted in orderly succession from the apostles, and remaining in*

---

[216] Ibid. 1:42.

> *the Churches to the present day, is still preserved, that alone is to be accepted as truth which differs in no respect from ecclesiastical and apostolic tradition.*[217]

Summing up the teachings of the apostles—the apostolic tradition—he draws the following Trinitarian summary:

> *The particular points clearly delivered in the teaching of the apostles are as follow: First, That there is one God, who created and arranged all things, and who, when nothing existed, called all things into being. ... Secondly, That Jesus Christ Himself, who came (into the world), was born of the Father before all creatures. ... Then, Thirdly, the apostles related that the Holy Spirit was associated in honour and dignity with the Father and the Son.*[218]

Cyprian of Carthage (210-258)

Although Cyprian did not directly attack the heresy of Adoptionism, he did attack the schism that was about to break the unity of his Church the same way Adoptionism was breaking the unity of God-man in Christ. Unity is the key-word here. For Cyprian, they were closely connected. The unity of the Church should reflect the unity found in the Trinity as well as the unity found in Christ. In his eyes, Christians gathering elsewhere, outside the Church, are scattering. As he put it,

> *There is one God, and Christ is one, and there is one Church, and one chair founded upon the rock by the word of the Lord. Another altar cannot be constituted nor a new priesthood be made, except the one altar and the one priesthood. Whosoever*

---

[217] De Principiis Preface 2.
[218] Ibid. Preface 4.

gathers elsewhere, scatters.[219]

The other heresy Cyprian had to cope with was Novatianism—claiming that people in grave sin were permanently excluded from the Church and were refused absolution. This heresy had become very significant after the bloody persecutions by emperors Decius and Valerian, when the Church had to face Christians who had "lapsed" by caving in to Roman pressure and agreeing to renounce their faith and offering sacrifice to the gods.

According to Novatianism, the Church of "Puritans" had no longer room for those who had "lapsed." But Cyprian was ready to welcome them back if they were willing to confess their sins and do penance. He was a voice of mercy after horrifying times of persecution. In his own words:

> *Cherish also by your presence the rest of the people who are lapsed, and cheer them by your consolation, that they may not fail of the faith and of God's mercy. For those shall not be forsaken by the aid and assistance of the Lord, who meekly, humbly, and with true penitence have persevered in good works; but the divine, remedy will be granted to them also. To the hearers also, if there are any overtaken by danger, and placed near to death, let your vigilance not be wanting; let not the mercy of the Lord be denied to those that are imploring the divine favour. I bid you, beloved brethren, ever heartily farewell; and remember me. Greet the whole brotherhood in my name, and remind them and ask them to be mindful of me. Farewell.*[220]

But Cyprian was not just white-washing their sin. He offered

---

[219] Epistles 39:5.
[220] Letters 12:2.

mercy, but at a price. Forgiveness can only be given to those who ask for it and repent. Therefore, he rebuffs mercy when "the combined temerity of certain of the lapsed, who refuse to repent and to make satisfaction to God, wrote to me, not asking that peace might be given to them, but claiming it as already given."[221] Mercy is a gift that cannot be demanded.

When Jesus said in the Gospel, "Your sins are forgiven," he only does so after repentance. Cyprian does the same for the lapsed:

> *It is time, therefore, that they should repent of their fault, that they should prove their grief for their lapse, that they should show modesty, that they should manifest humility, that they should exhibit some shame, that, by their submission, they should appeal to God's clemency for themselves, and by due honour for God's priest should draw forth upon themselves the divine mercy.*[222]

This is very different from what the heresy of Novatianism proclaims. Therefore, Cyprian's verdict about those who follow Novatian and actively spread his heresy is rather harsh:

> *And lest their raging boldness should ever cease, they are striving here also to distract the members of Christ into schismatical parties, and to cut and tear the one body of the Catholic Church, so that, running about from door to door, through the houses of many, or from city to city, through certain districts, they seek for companions in their obstinacy and error to join to themselves in their schism. To whom we have*

---

[221] Ibid. 28.
[222] Ibid. 29.

> *once given this reply, nor shall we cease to command them to lay aside their pernicious dissensions and disputes, and to be aware that it is an impiety to forsake their Mother; and to acknowledge and understand that when a bishop is once made and approved by the testimony and judgment of his colleagues and the people, another can by no means be appointed. Thus, if they consult their own interest peaceably and faithfully, if they confess themselves to be maintainers of the Gospel of Christ, they must return to the Church.*[223]

Obviously, unity is worth everything for Cyprian. He is willing to use all efforts to bring the "lapsed" back into the fold of the Church. Whereas those who have separated from the Church through heresy or schism *resist* the Church, the "lapsed," in stark contrast, *seek after* the Church. So Cyprian is actually inviting them back home:

> *[W]e recently sent our colleagues Caldonius and Fortunatus, that they might, not only by the persuasion of our letters, but by their presence and the advice of all of you, strive and labour with all their power to bring the members of the divided body into the unity of the Catholic Church, and associate them into the bond of Christian charity. But since the obstinate and inflexible pertinacity of the adverse party has not only rejected the bosom and the embrace of its root and Mother, but even, with a discord spreading and reviving itself worse and worse, has appointed a bishop for itself, and, contrary to the sacrament once delivered of the divine appointment and of Catholic Unity, has made an adulterous and opposed head outside the*

---

[223] Ibid. 40.

Church.[224]

For Cyprian, *permanent* separation from the Church in heresy or schism is more harmful than *temporary* weakness of the "lapsed" in times of tribulation. It is obvious to Cyprian that Novatianism, like any other heresy, is out to divide Christians and separate them from the Church and from the authority of the bishop:

> *For neither have heresies arisen, nor have schisms originated, from any other source than from this, that God's priest [bishop] is not obeyed; nor do they consider that there is one person for the time priest in the Church, and for the time judge in the stead of Christ; whom, if, according to divine teaching, the whole fraternity should obey, no one would stir up anything against the college of priests; no one, after the divine judgment, after the suffrage of the people, after the consent of the co-bishops, would make himself a judge, not now of the bishop, but of God. No one would rend the Church by a division of the unity of Christ.*[225]

There is a cosmic warfare going on, so to speak, between Good and Evil, between God and Satan. It is God's aim for each one of us to attain Heaven after death, whereas Satan's aim is to ensure that as many people as possible miss that eternal goal. Cyprian sees very clearly that it is the enemy of God we should be worried about:

> *He [Satan] has invented heresies and schisms, whereby he might subvert the faith, might corrupt the truth, might divide the unity. Those whom he cannot keep in the darkness of the old way, he circumvents and deceives by the error of*

---

[224] Ibid. 41:1.
[225] Ibid. 54:5.

a new way. He snatches men from the Church itself; and while they seem to themselves to have already approached to the light, and to have escaped the night of the world, he pours over them again, in their unconsciousness, new darkness; so that, although they do not stand firm with the Gospel of Christ, and with the observation and law of Christ, they still call themselves Christians, and, walking in darkness, they think that they have the light, while the adversary is flattering and deceiving, who, according to the apostle's word, transforms himself into an angel of light, and equips his ministers as if they were the ministers of righteousness, who maintain night instead of day, death for salvation, despair under the offer of hope, perfidy under the pretext of faith, antichrist under the name of Christ; so that, while they feign things like the truth, they make void the truth by their subtlety. This happens, beloved brethren, so long as we do not return to the source of truth, as we do not seek the head nor keep the teaching of the heavenly Master.[226]

The best guarantee we have for unity in the Church is the authority of the bishop, which gives each bishop an enormous responsibility. Each bishop shares this responsibility with other bishops for the benefit of the whole Church. This unity is comparable to the unity found in the images Cyprian uses—for instance, of a spring from which many streams flow:

And this unity we ought firmly to hold and assert, especially those of us that are bishops who preside in the Church, that we may also prove the episcopate itself to be one and undivided. Let no one deceive the brotherhood by a falsehood: let

---

[226] Treatises 1:3.

> *no one corrupt the truth of the faith by perfidious prevarication. The episcopate is one, each part of which is held by each one for the whole. The Church also is one, which is spread abroad far and wide into a multitude by an increase of fruitfulness. As there are many rays of the sun, but one light; and many branches of a tree, but one strength based in its tenacious root; and since from one spring flow many streams, although the multiplicity seems diffused in the liberality of an overflowing abundance, yet the unity is still preserved in the source.*[227]

"How can someone who does not hold this unity of the Church think that he holds the faith?"[228] For Cyprian, this is a rhetorical question. The unity of the Church is so essential to him that he even rejected the baptism performed by heretics. He considers baptism the sacrament of unity. Nowadays, we consider baptism valid, no matter in which church or denomination it was administered. But not so for Cyprian:

> *For it has been delivered to us, that there is one God, and one Christ, and one hope, and one faith, and one Church, and one baptism ordained only in the one Church, from which unity whosoever will depart must needs be found with heretics. ... he who was not in the ark of Noah could not be saved by water, so neither can he appear to be saved by baptism who has not been baptized in the Church which is established in the unity of the Lord according to the sacrament of the one ark.*[229]

The consequence of Cyprian's stand is that those who were

---

[227] Ibid. 1:5.
[228] Ibid. 1:4.
[229] Letters 73:11.

baptized by heretics must be baptized again "by the only and lawful baptism of the Church" when they come back to the one true Church. His argument is rather straightforward: "[I]f they are not in the Church, nay more, if they act against the Church, how can they baptize with the Church's baptism?"[230] Later on, Augustine of Hippo would express his confidence that Cyprian's beheading in 258 during persecution by Valerian atoned for his excesses during this conflict.[231]

Cyprian's extreme stance on this issue also made him coin one of his most famous statements in the history of Catholic theology: "there is no salvation out of the Church," [*extra ecclesiam nulla salus*], which was later rephrased as "outside the Church there is no salvation." First of all, we need to acknowledge that although Cyprian was the first to coin this expression, he did so in a very different context. It was his opinion that baptism performed by heretics, enemies of the Church, could not be valid. So those who are not in the Church—heretics, that is—cannot baptize with the Church's baptism. Cyprian was later condemned for this error.

However, his statement soon acquired a different meaning and became one of the most misunderstood teachings of the Catholic Church. It seems to suggest that people outside the Church can never be saved. Here is how the Catechism begins to address this topic: "How are we to understand this affirmation, often repeated by the Church Fathers? Reformulated positively, it means that all salvation comes from Christ the Head through the Church which is his Body."[232] Especially since Vatican II, the Church has "re-

---

[230] Ibid. 72:11.
[231] On Baptism, Against the Donatists 1:18.
[232] Catechism of the Catholic Church 846.

formulated" this teaching in a more positive way by acknowledging that not everyone may have had a "fair" chance to become acquainted with the Gospel, the Church, and her teachings. Although the document *Lumen Gentium* from Vatican II still confirms that those who have been given knowledge of Christ, but fail to act, "could not be saved," the Council also expressed,

> *Those who, through no fault of their own, do not know the Gospel of Christ or his Church, but who nevertheless seek God with a sincere heart, and, moved by grace, try in their actions to do his will as they know it through the dictates of their conscience—those too may achieve eternal salvation.*[233]

In other words, there is no salvation *without* Christ, but because this salvation has come to us through the Church, no salvation can come to us from *outside* the Church. So the mission of the Church remains to bring salvation within the reach of as many people as possible. Her message is not a declaration of universal salvation but a universal invitation to salvation—in an effort to make salvation as universal as possible. But again, that's not how Cyprian took his own statement.

After Cyprian had died, the validity of a sacrament became an even more extensive issue: if the validity of a sacrament could be suspended by schism, could it be suspended also by the sinfulness of the one who administered the sacrament? Church Father Augustine would address this problem a century later (see 9.c).

---

[233] Lumen Gentium, 16.

7. The 6th Generation (280-330)

a. Backdrop

A time of ups and downs was lying ahead for Christians. In 260, Valerius' son Gallienus (260-268) had taken over as emperor. It came as a complete surprise that this man would ease up on the Christians. He formally decreed that from now on Christians could worship freely, own property, and even hold office. But soon, two other bloody persecutions would take place during the reign of emperors Diocletian (284-305) and Gallerius (305-311). However, by the beginning of the 4th century, the failure of the persecutions was even evident to the emperors. Emperor Gallerius would switch tactics and issued an Edict of Toleration in 311.

Although it was a bad time for the empire as a whole—with some 25 different emperors in 50 years—a dream had come true for Christians. Basilicas began to go up for the first time in history. Christians could work their way up through the ranks in the military and the government. The Church was expanding. In 260, there were about one million Christians in the empire, but by the year 300, their number had grown to six million—making up about 10 to 15 percent of the total population. Nevertheless, Christians were still despised and not really trusted by many. Their life style was too different from what was accepted and expected.

However, there is always also a dark side to living in peace—

laxity sets in, even among Christians. The records of the Council of Elvira, Spain, in 300 paint a rather dark picture. They list a catalogue that mentions money-grabbing bishops, loan-sharking pastors, deacons participating in pagan worship, and laypersons who went through adultery, abortion, and divorce. All of this may not sound too unfamiliar to modern ears. Yet, the Church was expanding.

Not only was the Church expanding, but so was the empire. The Roman Empire had grown but had also come under attack from enemies outside its borders. Its territory had become too large to be ruled by one man alone. So in 284, Emperor Diocletian decided to reorganize the empire and divide it into two parts, East and West, each one further divided into half. So there would be four emperors. But another outcome of this division was that, very soon, only a few in the western part could read Greek, and no one in the eastern part bothered to learn Latin. The line was drawn and would leave an impact for centuries to come.

During this time, the empire was decaying from the inside as well. In general, the empire itself was not a bad institution—as G. K. Chesterton put it, "It was the best thing the world had yet seen." The *Pax Romana* had united the world and had created stability. But the Roman Empire was also running dry. Belief in the old gods was dissipating. There was nothing more to conquer and nothing left to do but live on bread alone—that is, bread and games. This void had created space for an enormous immorality: the pleasure of sexual perversion, the cruelty of bloody gladiatorial combats, the performance of abortion, the spread of venereal diseases, and the list was growing.

As to bloody spectacles in arenas, the 6th generation Church Father Lactantius (see 7.c) once made a striking comparison between victims, perpetrators, and spectators:

> *[If] the spectator is involved in the same guilt as the perpetrator, then in these slaughters of gladiators, he who is a spectator is no less sprinkled with blood than he who sheds it; nor can he be free from the guilt of bloodshed who wished it to be poured out, or appear not to have slain, who both favoured the slayer and asked a reward for him.*[234]

Indeed, the pagans had a culture of death, whereas the Christians had a culture of life. So something had to change, or else the empire itself would be under a death threat too. The emperor knew it and felt it. That's when Emperor Diocletian went into action. He saw this strange movement, the Catholic Church, as a rival force inside the Roman Empire—a threat to the very existence of his empire and its unity. So a new edict was decreed for all parts of the empire, which would drastically turn the tide for Christians: all Christian buildings were to be destroyed, sacred Scriptures and liturgical vessels seized, and meetings forbidden. Christians had to surrender their religious treasures. Although some of them handed over only heretical volumes or even medical books to police—making it look like they were obeying the edict—this was also the time when many valuable Christian manuscripts got lost for future generations.

Diocletian's great tribulation of 303 went on for eight full years. It became known as the "Great Persecution," worse than any of the nine previous persecutions. Some of the more famous martyrs of this time period are Agnes, Agatha, Lucy, and the Forty Martyrs of Sebaste.

---

[234] Epitome of the Divine Institutes 63.

Lactantius, a Church Father of this generation, actually questioned the perpetrators of these persecutions. How can they be just and pious if their victims are considered desperate and impious?

> *I should wish to know, when they compel men to sacrifice against their will, what reasoning they have with themselves, or to whom they make that offering. ... If it is a good to which you call me, why do you invite me with evil? Why with blows, and not with words? Why not by argument, but by bodily tortures? Whence it is manifest that that is an evil, to which you do not allure me willing, but drag me refusing. What folly is it to wish to consult the good of any one against his will! ... What perversity is this, that he who is punished, though innocent, should be called desperate and impious, and that the torturer, on the other hand, should be called just and pious!*[235]

b. Trouble Within: Modalism | Patripassianism

In times of trouble, the Church usually also experiences trouble from within. For this generation, the trouble was Modalism. Modalism had been around for a while, but it kept popping up its ugly head. Modalism was the belief of two notable early Church figures, Praxeas and Sabellius, both of whom aroused a large following in the Church in the late 2nd (Praxeas) and early 3rd century (Sabellius). Together they promoted a heresy that is usually called Modalism. Modalism has been mainly associated with Sabellius—hence the name Sabellianism—who taught a form of it in Rome in the 3rd century. The idea behind it had come to him via the teachings of Praxeas.

---

[235] Ibid. 53.

Modalism is the theory that God is one, not three. God is one Person who has revealed himself in three forms or "modes"—hence, the name Modalism. God only *appears* to be three because at different times he takes on a different role—first Father, then Son, then Holy Spirit. God is forever one. What orthodox Christians call "Trinity" simply consists of three successive roles played by the same supreme God over the course of salvation history. This heresy confirms God's omnipresence, and his ability to manifest himself as he pleases. Thus, Modalism reduces the Trinity to a divine show; God is said to have three "faces" or "masks." This makes the Trinity look like we look at water, which remains the same substance even though it can appear as a liquid, a solid, and a gas.

If that comparison were true, then this would obscure the individual reality of the three divine Persons, for water cannot exist in all three forms at once. Put differently, during the Incarnation, according to Modalism, Jesus was simply God acting in one mode or role, and the Holy Spirit at Pentecost was God acting in a different mode. Thus, God does not exist as the Father, Son, and Holy Spirit at the same time. Rather, he is one Person and has merely manifested himself in these three modes at various times. Modalism thus denies the basic distinctiveness and coexistence of the three Persons of the Trinity.

A heresy connected with Modalism is Patripassianism (or Patripassionism): it is the Father [*pater*] himself who suffers on the Cross [*passio*]. It asserts that God the Father—rather than God the Son—became incarnate and suffered on the Cross for our redemption. When the Son suffered, it was actually God who experienced the sufferings. When Jesus was in pain, God himself was in pain. When Jesus died on the Cross, God died on the Cross. This means that it was

God, in playing the "Son role" while Jesus was on earth, who actually suffered and died on the cross.

If this were true, then the Son's suffering as God would mean that he experienced our human suffering in a mitigated divine manner, and thus that he did not experience suffering as human beings do experience suffering. Put in Trinitarian terminology, to place the significance of the Son's suffering within his *divine* nature is to relegate his *human* suffering to insignificance, and thus to demote all human suffering to insignificance. Ironically, those who advocate a "suffering God" have actually locked suffering within God's divine nature, and thus have locked God out of all human suffering. So when Jesus died on the Cross, it was not Jesus but God himself dying on the Cross.

Is Modalism still alive today? Present day groups that hold forms of the heresy of Modalism are the Oneness Pentecostal, United Pentecostal, and United Apostolic Churches. They are often referred to as churches of the "Jesus Only" theology since they claim that Jesus is the only person in the Godhead and that the Father, the Son, and the Holy Spirit are merely names, modes, or roles of Jesus. Heresies are hard to kill; they keep coming back over and over again. One could even state that the rather recent God-is-dead theology is in essence an outcome of this heresy.[236]

c. Defenders of the Faith

Lactantius (240-320)

Lactantius was born a pagan and in his early life taught rhetoric in his native place in North Africa. So gifted was this man that at the request of Emperor Diocletian, he became an

---

[236] This theology was promoted by theologians such as Thomas J. J. Altizer, Paul van Buren, and Anglican Bishop John Robinson.

official professor of rhetoric in Nicomedia, present-day Turkey. But after he had converted to Christianity, Diocletian promulgated his "Edict against the Christians" in 303, which started another bloody persecution. Obviously, Lactantius could not retain his position as public teacher, so he lived in poverty for a while.

In most of his writings, Lactantius wants to speak to people who have a pagan background and are at best familiar with pagan philosophers, but have only very basic knowledge of Christianity and its teachings. Most questions he addresses are related to the seeming inconsistency of Christian teachings—such as "one God with three Persons," and Jesus being "truly God and truly man" at the same time. These were inconsistencies or contradictions that heresies tried to eliminate, but that Lactantius wanted to protect and explain.

Lactantius wants to make very clear to his readers that the heresy of Modalism makes God "one" without acknowledging the "three" in God, and makes Jesus "one" without acknowledging the "two" in him. For that reason, Modalism needs to be rejected, but only after some clear explanations and distinctions for the readers whom Lactantius always keeps in mind:

> *When we speak of God the Father and God the Son, we do not speak of them as different, nor do we separate each: because the Father cannot exist without the Son, nor can the Son be separated from the Father, since the name of Father cannot be given without the Son, nor can the Son be begotten without the Father. Since, therefore, the Father makes the Son, and the Son the Father, they both have one mind, one spirit, one substance; but the former is as it were an overflowing fountain, the latter as a stream flowing forth from it: the former as the sun, the*

> *latter as it were a ray extended from the sun. And since He is both faithful to the Most High Father, and beloved by Him, He is not separated from Him; just as the stream is not separated from the fountain, nor the ray from the sun: for the water of the fountain is in the stream, and the light of the sun is in the ray: just as the voice cannot be separated from the mouth, nor the strength or hand from the body.[237]*

Unlike heretics, Lactantius preserves the tension and paradox of the Christian Faith: the Son and the Father are one God, for the one is as two, and the two are as one, but not in the way Modalism portrays this:

> *For since the Father loves the Son, and gives all things to Him, and the Son faithfully obeys the Father, and wills nothing except that which the Father does, it is plain that so close a relationship cannot be separated, so that they should be said to be two in whom there is but one substance, and will, and faith. Therefore the Son is through the Father, and the Father through the Son. One honour is to be given to both, as to one God, and is to be so divided through the worship of the two, that the division itself may be bound by an inseparable bond of union.[238]*

> *But, however, that it might be certain that He was sent by God, it was befitting that He should not be born as man is born, composed of a mortal on both sides; but that it might appear that He was heavenly even in the form of man, He was born without the office of a father. For He had a spiritual Father, God; and as God was the Father of His spirit without a mother, so a virgin was the mother of His body without a*

---

[237] Divine Institutes 4:29.
[238] Epitome of the Divine Institutes 49.

> *father. He was therefore both God and man, being placed in the middle between God and man. From which the Greeks call Him Mesites, that He might be able to lead man to God—that is, to immortality: for if He had been God only (as we have before said), He would not have been able to afford to man examples of goodness; if He had been man only, He would not have been able to compel men to righteousness, unless there had been added an authority and virtue greater than that of man.[239]*

There are many more questions. How can the Son of God be born as a man? In what sense was the Son "fatherless" and "motherless"? Was Jesus the Son of God or the Son of man? Lactantius uses his philosophical mind to explain this mystery as much as possible for non-Christians:

> *Nevertheless it was His pleasure that He should be born as a man, that in all things He might be like His supreme Father. For God the Father Himself, who is the origin and source of all things, inasmuch as He is without parents, is most truly named by Trismegistus fatherless and motherless, because He was born from no one. For which reason it was befitting that the Son also should be twice born, that He also might become fatherless and motherless. For in His first nativity, which was spiritual, He was motherless, because He was begotten by God the Father alone, without the office of a mother. But in His second, which was in the flesh, He was born of a virgin's womb without the office of a father, that, bearing a middle substance between God and man, He might be able, as it were, to take by the hand this frail and weak nature of ours, and raise it to immortality. He became both the Son*

---

[239] Divine Institutes 4:25.

> *of God through the Spirit, and the Son of man through the flesh—that is, both God and man.*[240]

The scandal of God becoming man and accepting human suffering is actually seen by Lactantius as "a great and divine plan." In this way he combats the heresy of Patripassianism:

> *I come now to the passion itself, which is often cast in our teeth as a reproach: that we worship a man, and one who was visited and tormented with remarkable punishment: that I may show that this very passion was undergone by Him in accordance with a great and divine plan, and that goodness and truth and wisdom are contained in it alone. For if He had been most happy on the earth, and had reigned through all His life in the greatest prosperity, no wise man would either have believed Him to be a God, or judged Him worthy of divine honour.*[241]

Why did he not come as purely God to teach us? Why did the immortal one become mortal and undergo suffering? These are legitimate questions pagans as well as Christians have. Lactantius deems them worthy a serious answer:

> *They say, in short, that it was unworthy of God to be willing to become man, and to burden Himself with the infirmity of flesh; to become subject of His own accord to sufferings, to pain, and death. ... Why, then (they say), did He not come as God to teach men? Why did He render Himself so humble and weak, that it was possible for Him both to be despised by men and to be visited with punishment? Why did He suffer violence from those who are weak and mortal? Why did He not repel by strength, or avoid by*

---

[240] Ibid. 4:13.
[241] Ibid. 4:16.

> *His divine knowledge, the hands of men? Why did He not at least in His very death reveal His majesty?*[242]

What is the answer to such questions? Since Jesus is truly God and truly man, he can be more than an earthly, imperfect teacher, namely also a heavenly, perfect teacher at the same time. If he wasn't heavenly and divine, his teaching would always remain imperfect and the salvation he gained for us would be powerless. In the words of Lactantius:

> *Hence it comes to pass, that an earthly teacher cannot be perfect. But a teacher from heaven, to whom His divine nature gives knowledge, and His immortality gives virtue, must of necessity in His teaching also, as in other things, be perfect and complete. But this cannot by any means happen, unless He should take to Himself a mortal body. And the reason why it cannot happen is manifest. For if He should come to men as God, not to mention that mortal eyes cannot look upon and endure the glory of His majesty in His own person, assuredly God will not be able to teach virtue; for, inasmuch as He is without a body, He will not practice the things which He will teach, and through this His teaching will not be perfect.*[243]

This has serious consequences for the heresy of Patripassianism. If Jesus only suffered as a *divine* being, his teaching would have been useless for *human* beings. Jesus is God, but God is not Jesus. With Jesus' suffering, the Son of God was in pain, but God the Father was in charge. What we need is a "God-in-charge," not a "God-in-pain." Lactantius saw the problem very clearly:

---

[242] Ibid. 4:22.
[243] Ibid. 4:24.

> *It is befitting that a master and teacher of virtue should most closely resemble man, that by overpowering sin he may teach man that sin may be overpowered by him. But if he is immortal, he can by no means propose an example to man. For there will stand forth some one persevering in his opinion, and will say: You indeed do not sin, because you are free from this body; you do not covet, because nothing is needed by an immortal; but I have need of many things for the support of this life. You do not fear death, because it can have no power against you. You despise pain, because you can suffer no violence. But I, a mortal, fear both, because they bring upon me the severest tortures, which the weakness of the flesh cannot endure. ... You see, therefore, how much more perfect is a teacher who is mortal, because he is able to be a guide to one who is mortal, than one who is immortal, for he is unable to teach patient endurance who is not subject to passions.*[244]

Lactantius presents all of this, counter to all heresies, as the only true Faith which can be found in the Catholic Church alone:

> *For when they are called Phrygians, or Novatians, or Valentinians, or Marcionites, or Anthropians, or Arians, or by any other name, they have ceased to be Christians, who have lost the name of Christ, and assumed human and external names. Therefore it is the Catholic Church alone which retains true worship.*[245]

Alexander of Alexandria (c. 250-327)

This Church Father, Alexander, is best known for his battle

---

[244] Ibid. 4:24.
[245] Ibid. 4:30.

against Arianism, which is in fact the subject of the next chapter. But because he was already old when that battle came to a head, he was basically part of an older generation, the 6th generation in our "pedigree," and that's why he is mentioned in this chapter, as a precursor of what is coming.

In a sense, Arianism—which we will explain later in more detail—is a heresy that has some similarity to Modalism. Both heresies make an exclusive choice and break the tension. Modalists break the paradox of God being one and yet being three—so they give God three different roles. Arians break the paradox of Jesus being truly human and yet being truly divine—so they eliminate one of them, his divinity. They claim that there was a time when the Son of God was not the Son of God.

Alexander combats relentlessly this idea that there was a time when the Son of God was *not* the Son of God:

> *I have stirred myself up to show you the faithlessness of these men who say that there was a time when the Son of God was not; and that He who was not before, came into existence afterwards, becoming such, when at length He was made, even as every man is wont to be born. For, they say, God made all things from things which are not, comprehending even the Son of God in the creation of all things rational and irrational. To which things they add as a consequence, that He is of mutable nature, and capable both of virtue and vice. And this hypothesis being once assumed, that He is from things which are not, they overturn the sacred writings concerning His eternity, which signify the immutability and the Godhead of Wisdom*

and the Word, which are Christ.[246]

Alexander also touches on something the heresy of Adoptionism claims, namely that God had chosen the man Jesus as his Son (see 6.b). He explains clearly what its heresy is:

> *[T]hey, throwing off all religious reverence, say that God, since He foreknew and had foreseen that His Son would not rebel against Him, chose Him from all. For He did not choose Him as having by nature anything specially beyond His other sons, for no one is by nature a son of God, as they say; neither as having any peculiar property of His own; but God chose Him who was of a mutable nature, on account of the carefulness of His manners and His practice, which in no way turned to that which is evil; so that, if Paul and Peter had striven for this, there would have been no difference between their sonship and His.*[247]

In defiance of Modalism and Sabellianism, Alexander expresses his adherence to what the Apostolic Church proclaims. Her belief is very clear and orthodox:

> *In one Father unbegotten, who has from no one the cause of His being, who is unchangeable and immutable, who is always the same, and admits of no increase or diminution; who gave to us the Law, the prophets, and the Gospels; who is Lord of the patriarchs and apostles, and all the saints. And in one Lord Jesus Christ, the only-begotten Son of God; not begotten of things which are not, but of Him who is the Father; not in a corporeal manner, by excision or division as Sabellius and*

---

[246] Epistles of Arianism 1:2.
[247] Ibid. 1:3.

> *Valentinus thought, but in a certain inexplicable and unspeakable manner ... for in our ears are sounding the words before uttered by Christ on this very thing, No man knows the Father, save the Son; and no man knows who the Son is, save the Father. ... in this alone is He inferior to the Father, that He is not unbegotten. For He is the very exact image of the Father, and in nothing differing from Him.*[248]

In response to the heresy of Patripassianism, he declares that the man Jesus came down from Heaven and suffered so we could live forever because he was also God:

> *Therefore God sent down from heaven His incorporeal Son to take flesh upon Him in the Virgin's womb; and thus, equally as you, was He made man; to save lost man, and collect all His scattered members. For Christ, when the joined the manhood to His person, united that which death by the separation of the body had dispersed. Christ suffered that we should live for ever.*[249]

Alexander is not afraid to pose some pertinent questions that many Christians would ask: why did Jesus become man; why did Jesus die?

> *For else why should Christ have died? Had He committed anything worthy of death? Why did He clothe Himself in flesh who was invested with glory? And since He was God, why did He become man? And since He reigned in heaven, why did He come down to earth, and become incarnate in the virgin's womb? What necessity, I ask, impelled God to come down to earth, to assume flesh, to be wrapped in swaddling clothes*

---

[248] Ibid. 1:12.
[249] Ibid. 1:5:5.

> *in a manger-cradle, to be nourished with the milk from the breast, to receive baptism from a servant, to be lifted up upon the cross, to be interred in an earthly sepulchre, to rise again the third day from the dead? What necessity, I say, impelled Him to this?*[250]

He gave the answer in one sentence: "He suffered shame for man's sake, to set him free from death."[251] Yet, God coming down from Heaven, to become man and to suffer in order to heal our sufferings, remains a *mystery*:

> *Oh, the new and ineffable mystery! The Judge was judged. He who absolves from sin was bound; He was mocked who once framed the world; He was stretched upon the cross who stretched out the heavens; He was fed with gall who gave the manna to be bread; He died who gives life. He was given up to the tomb who raises the dead. ... For our Lord was made man; He was condemned that He might impart compassion; He was bound that He might set free; He was apprehended that He might liberate; He suffered that He might heal our sufferings; He died to restore life to us; He was buried to raise us up. For when our Lord suffered, His humanity suffered, that which He had like man.*[252]

But it is crucial to keep in mind that, when the Lord Jesus suffered, it was his humanity that suffered—not his divinity, as Patripassianism had erroneously proclaimed. And God was certainly not playing the role of Jesus in a manner Modalism had portrayed. Alexander, bishop and patriarch of Alexandria, felt very strongly his role and mission of keeping the Apostolic Faith pure and clean, based on tradition and

---

[250] Ibid. 1:5:5.
[251] Ibid. 1:5:5.
[252] Ibid. 1:6.

the apostolic succession. No wonder, he was a key figure in Church history—a very important and strong chain connecting the 6th generation with the 7th generation of Church Fathers. He merely was passing on what the apostles had passed on before him, six generations ago. And he in turn was passing on what he had received to the 7th generation.

8. The 7th Generation (330-380)

a. Backdrop

While in the Eastern part of the empire blood was still flowing on a daily basis, hope was coming for Christians from the western half of the empire. When the emperor of the West, Constantius, died in Britain in 306, his army hailed his son Constantine as the new emperor. There was Christian influence in his family somewhere, for Constantine had a half-sister named Anastasia, which means "Resurrection."

When Constantine's co-emperor, Maxentius, declared war to Constantine, after building an army in Italy of over 100,000 troops, Constantine decided, although he had fewer than 40,000 troops, not to wait but attack him on his own territory. After a chain of stunning victories, Constantine found himself across the Tiber from Rome. That's when he had a vision of God showing him a symbol—an X [*Chi*] with a P [*Rho*] superimposed on it, known to Christians as the first two Greek letters of the word *Christ*—and telling him to make this his standard. Constantine emblazoned this Christian emblem on banners and on the shields of his soldiers. He knew that under this sign, he would be victorious—and that he was. Rome's citizens hailed him as their liberator. The Western half of the empire had its first Christian emperor.

Was he really a Christian? Not in the strict sense, but at least he was very sympathetic to the Christians. He did mint coins that contained the Chi-Rho symbol. He did promulgate, together with the new emperor of the Eastern half, Licinius, a world-wide decree, known as the Edict of Milan, which allowed all citizens of the entire empire to follow their religious beliefs in peace. This edict changed Christianity from a persecuted to an officially favored religion. Also did Constantine give a large property from the Lateran family to the Church for the construction of a basilica and residence of the pope—called to this very day St. John Lateran. In addition, he did erect a basilica over the tomb of St. Peter on the hill across the Tiber known as the Vatican. And when Licinius began to harass Christians again in the East, Constantine took military action, defeated him, and thus became the sole ruler of the Roman Empire in both East and West.

Constantine had always hoped Christianity would help him unify his empire—and in fact it did—but soon he would realize the roles would need to be reversed too: the empire would need to help unify Christianity because there was a new rift lurking at the horizon of the Church, and therefore indirectly of the empire. Its name was Arianism.

But times would change, as they always do. A new emperor from 361 to 363—called Julian and soon to be known as "Julian the Apostate"—would be the next key player in the history of the Church. In his *Church History*, Theodoret (c. 393- c. 458) tells us how Julian went astray:

> *Now Julian flung away the apprehensions which had previously stood him in good stead, and, moved by unrighteous confidence, set his heart on seizing the sceptre of empire. Accordingly, on his way through Greece, he sought out seers and soothsayers, with a desire of learning if he should*

> *get what his soul longed for. He met with a man who promised to predict these things, conducted him into one of the idol temples, introduced him within the shrine, and called upon the demons of deceit.*[253]

Those demons did a good job. Once emperor, Julian ordered the pagan temples to be re-opened, victims to be brought to the altars for sacrifice, churches to be wrecked, and the worship of the gods to be restored. He always referred to Christians as "Galileans," in order to avoid saying the word Christ. He officially published his plans to reorganize the various pagan priesthoods into some kind of a "real pagan church," with "archpriests" and he himself as Pontifex Maximus over all. In doing so, he finished the transition from Christianity through Arianism back to paganism.

b. Trouble Within: Arianism

Beginning in 313, Arius had been building quite a following in one of the most prestigious churches in Egypt, which was given to him by bishop Alexander of Alexandria, of all people. His message seemed indeed quite orthodox—God is one—but then he veered off in a heterodox direction—if God is one, then Jesus can't be God as well. He admitted that Jesus is the incarnation of the Word, directly created by God, but God made the Word first, out of nothing, so that he could use him to make everything else. Since the Son was created out of nothing, like everything else, there obviously was a time when he was *not*. If the Father begot the Son, then he that was begotten must have had a beginning of existence. So there had to be a time when the Son was not the Son. He had to be created at some point.

Arius insisted that the Son is a creature made by God and is

---

[253] Ecclesiastical History 3:1.

thus subject to change and imperfection—which means that Jesus was someone other than and less that God, did not have full and accurate knowledge of God, and that the Incarnation was not the full reconciliation between God and humanity that it seemed. Since the Father is utterly transcendent, the Son can't really know him as he truly is, neither can he reveal the Father to us. He is only called "Son" by virtue of adoption. Adoptionism was back in the picture. Whereas the heresy of Docetism had denied Jesus' true humanity, the heresy of Arianism denied his true divinity.

Arianism appears so clear, simple, and logical that it becomes very attractive. First it assumes that Christ really is a son in the regular sense, by insisting that no son is as old as his own father. But then it turns things around by using this premise to conclude that Christ is no son at all, except in an analogous way. From there, it makes tiny, persuading logical steps: if Jesus is Son, then he was begotten; if he is begotten, then he had a beginning; if he had a beginning, then he is not infinite; if he is not infinite, then he is not God. In logic and math, that would be followed by *Quod erat demonstrandum* (QED). It is as simple as that!

Apparently, for Arius, the terms "begotten" and "created" should be considered synonymous, which is very questionable. C. S. Lewis explains the difference between "begotten" and "created" lucidly, as only he can:

> *To beget is to become the father of: to create is to make. And the difference is this. When you beget, you beget something of the same kind as yourself. ... But when you make, you make something of a different kind than yourself. ... What God begets is God; just as what man begets is man. What God creates is not God; just as*

what man makes is not man.[254]

In spite of twists and spins like this, Arius knew how to take his Arianism to the streets. He was a master in gathering priests and deacons, even bishops, to support his case. Thus from a little spark a large fire was kindled, spreading swiftly from its origin in Alexandria to the rest of the world. It would spread throughout all of Egypt, and soon over Asia Minor. One of its strongest points was that it could get "Christianity" more easily accepted by a wide variety of otherwise hesitant Roman citizens. Arianism is a clever attempt to allow us to go on worshipping a creature—a merely human Jesus, a prophet, or wise man at best—rather than the Creator. The outcome amounts basically to centuries-old paganism.

In a way, Arianism makes the same mistake as Modalism. They both break the mysterious tension of "God is one, yet God is three" and "Jesus is human, yet Jesus is divine" by making a choice—remember, the word heresy means "choice"—and eliminating one of the two sides of the paradox.

Alexander of Alexandria, the legendary foe of Arianism, describes the Arian heresy as a long litany of denials:

> *God was not always the Father; but there was a time when God was not the Father. The Word of God was not always, but was made 'from things that are not;' for He who is God fashioned the non-existing from the non-existing; wherefore there was a time when He was not. For the Son is a thing created, and a thing made: nor is He like to the Father in substance; nor is He the true and natural Word of the Father; nor is He His true Wisdom; but He is one of the things fashioned*

---

[254] Lewis, C.S. *Mere Christianity*, book 4, chapter 1.

> *and made. And He is called, by a misapplication of the terms, the Word and Wisdom, since He is Himself made by the proper Word of God, and by that wisdom which is in God, in which, as God made all other things, so also did He make Him. Wherefore, He is by His very nature changeable and mutable, equally with other rational beings. The Word, too, is alien and separate from the substance of God. The father also is ineffable to the Son; for neither does the Word perfectly and accurately know the Father, neither can He perfectly see Him. For neither does the Son indeed know His own substance as it is. Since He for our sakes was made, that by Him as by an instrument God might create us; nor would He have existed had not God wished to make us.*[255]

Alexander had been the first one to deal with Arius' teaching and to sense his error. In 320, almost near the end of his life, he called a meeting of the bishops of Egypt and surrounding areas. Eighty out of the approximately one hundred who gathered agreed to excommunicate Arius if he did not retract his heretical teaching. But Arius refused and fled to Nicomedia in present-day Turkey, where he began drumming up support from other bishops in the surrounding areas.

As Patriarch of Alexandria, Alexander sent a letter to his colleague Alexander, the bishop of the City of Constantinople, to warn him for Arianism:

> *[I]n order that you may be aware of such men, lest any of them presume to set foot in your dioceses, whether by themselves or by others; for these sorcerers know how to use hypocrisy to carry out their fraud; and to employ letters*

---

[255] Epistles on Arianism 2:2.

> *composed and dressed out with lies, which are able to deceive a man who is intent upon a simple and sincere faith. Arius, therefore, and Achilles, having lately entered into a conspiracy, emulating the ambition of Colluthus, have turned out far worse than he. For Colluthus, indeed, who reprehends these very men, found some pretext for his evil purpose; but these, beholding his battering of Christ, endured no longer to be subject to the Church; but building for themselves dens of thieves, they hold their assemblies in them unceasingly, night and day directing their calumnies against Christ and against us. For since they call in question all pious and doctrine, after the manner of the Jews, they have constructed a workshop for contending against Christ, denying the Godhead of our Saviour, and preaching that He is only the equal of all others.*[256]

In spite of Alexander's efforts, the heresy kept spreading. Arius had fled to Nicomedia where Emperor Constantine had his imperial palace. When Constantine heard of the new heresy, he initially wondered what all the commotion was about, but he was soon informed more accurately by a bishop friend. So he summoned a large assembly of bishops to resolve the matter in the nearby city of Nicaea.

The date set for the opening convocation was, according to most historians, May 20, 325. The scene was something to behold: to see not only so many bishops, but also those bishops who had been victims of previous persecutions—in the words of Theodoret:

> *Paul, bishop of Neo-Cæsarea, a fortress situated on the banks of the Euphrates, had suffered from*

---

[256] Ibid. 1:1.

> *the frantic rage of Licinius. He had been deprived of the use of both hands by the application of a red-hot iron, by which the nerves which give motion to the muscles had been contracted and rendered dead. Some had had the right eye dug out, others had lost the right arm. Among these was Paphnutius of Egypt. In short, the Council looked like an assembled army of martyrs.[257]*

Never before had a council of bishops been convened by a Christian emperor. Never before had the government paid for the travelling costs of the attendees. What had never been done before by a Council either was that the attending bishops—between 250 and 300—expressed Church teaching by drafting a Creed that all were bound to accept.

The bishops took a local baptismal creed and edited it so carefully and precisely that the divinity of Christ was clearly defined, thus ruling out the heresy of Arianism. At the end, they added,

> *But those who say: 'There was a time when he was not;' and 'He was not before he was made;' and 'He was made out of nothing,' or 'He is of another substance' or 'essence,' or 'The Son of God is created,' or 'changeable,' or 'alterable'— they are condemned by the holy catholic and apostolic Church.[258]*

To rule out any Arian interpretation of their Creed, the council fathers decided to introduce two technical terms not found in Scripture—*ousia* ("being" or "substance") and *homoousios* ("consubstantial" or "of the same substance")— to make utterly clear that the Father and the Son are equally

---

[257] Ecclesiastical History 1:6.
[258] The Nicene Creed we use nowadays in most Sunday Masses is a later, slightly expanded version crafted at the Council of Constantinople in 381.

divine. Although some had reservations about the term *homoousios*, everyone put their signature on the Creed, except Arius and two of his most ardent supporters.

Hence, Emperor Constantine wrote to all the churches of the empire, "the judgment of three hundred bishops cannot be other than the judgment of God." Arius and the two diehards—about one percent of the delegates who attended Nicaea—were exiled. Church unity had been restored. Later on, Church Father Theodore of Mopsuestia (350-428) would explain that the phrase "'homoousios' or 'consubstantial' with the Father" is not different from that of "true God of true God." But let there be no misunderstanding: Nicaea did not attempt to explain the mystery of the Son of God that Arius had been trying to remove; instead, it left the paradoxes of the Son of God as paradoxical as it had found them.

It has been noted that the Greek term *homoousios* or "consubstantial", which Athanasius of Alexandria had favored, was known to have been put forth by Sabellius, which was something that many followers of Athanasius were uneasy about. Their objection to the term was that it was considered to be not only un-Scriptural, but also "of a Sabellian tendency." Nevertheless, the Nicaean Creed was overwhelming accepted as Church orthodoxy.

Some have raised a few critical or even skeptical questions about the outcome of Nicaea: Did the emperor certify the outcome of the Nicene Council? Was the Creed a creation of Constantine? Athanasius later vehemently denied these suggestions when he wrote,

> *When did a judgment of the Church receive its validity from the Emperor? Or rather when was his decree ever recognised by the Church? There*

> *have been many Councils held heretofore; and many judgments passed by the Church; but the Fathers never sought the consent of the Emperor thereto, nor did the Emperor busy himself with the affairs of the Church. The Apostle Paul had friends among them of Cæsar's household, and in his Epistle to the Philippians he sent salutations from them; but he never took them as his associates in Ecclesiastical judgments.*[259]

Not surprisingly, Arius himself also attacked the use of the term *homoousios* as foreign to Scripture. But Athanasius replied by showing that Arius and his followers also had used terms not found in Scripture, such as "Jesus was created out of nothing" and "there was a time when Christ was not." So he wrote against the Arians in response,

> *And their murmuring, that the phrases are unscriptural, is exposed as vain by themselves, for they have uttered their impieties in unscriptural terms: (for such are 'of nothing' and 'there was a time when He was not'), while yet they find fault because they were condemned by unscriptural terms pious in meaning. ... the Bishops, not having invented their phrases for themselves, but having testimony from their Fathers, wrote as they did.*[260]

Nevertheless, after Nicaea, the case would still be far from settled. Arianism remained strong for a while and was a real rival for the orthodox Faith. Besides, it had many serious, dangerous implications. One of them was this: if Jesus is not God but merely a human being, then his words and actions are worth as much, or rather as little, as anyone else's. Another one was perhaps even more detrimental: if Jesus

---

[259] History of the Arians 7:52.
[260] Ad Afros Epistula Synodica 6.

The First Christians: Keeping the Faith in Times of Trouble

was only *like* God, then someone else even *more* like God might arise somewhere. If that is true, then Jesus was only an interim rather than a definitive revelation of God. If so, then the revealed truth so far might be less than that of later arrivals. If so, then all of Jesus statements and commandments would have only temporary value. This would be contrary to what the apostles and the Church had affirmed over and over again—that Jesus was the definitive Word of God, that he was fully God and fully man, and that his teaching, life, death and Resurrection were definitive, not interim, revelations from God.

So there were some serious problems with Arianism. But don't think Arianism is something of the past. It is still alive in some form today—not only inside Christianity in branches such as Unitarianism, but also outside Christianity in a religion such as Islam, which only emerged some three centuries later while Arianism was still very much alive. We shouldn't forget that the Christians Mohammed knew were Arians, or had at least been affected by Arian doctrines. The late historian Hilaire Belloc gave the following description of Islam:

> *But the central point where this new heresy struck home with a mortal blow against Catholic tradition was a full denial of the Incarnation. Mohammed did not merely take the first steps toward that denial, as the Arians and their followers had done; he advanced a clear affirmation, full and complete, against the whole doctrine of an incarnate God. He taught that Our Lord was the greatest of all the prophets, but still only a prophet: a man like other men. He eliminated the Trinity altogether ... So true is this that today very few men, even among those who are highly instructed in history, recall the truth*

> *that Mohammedanism was essentially in its origins not a new religion, but a heresy.*[261]

One of the first times we hear about the link between Islam and Arianism is in the writings of a later Church Father John of Damascus (675-749). In his work *Fountain of Knowledge* he writes, "From that time to the present a false prophet named Mohammed has appeared in their midst. This man, after having chanced upon the Old and New Testaments and likewise, it seems, having conversed with an Arian monk, devised his own heresy."[262] John of Damascus was convinced that Islam was in essence not a separate religion, but instead a heretical form of Christianity. Mohammed did not learn much from Christianity, but he did get the gist of Arianism: Jesus is not God. Not surprisingly, the areas of the Roman Empire where Arianism had been popular were now wide open to Islam.

The case could even be made that Eastern Christian practice formed the template for what were to become the basic conventions of Islam. The Muslim form of prayer with its bowings and prostrations is strikingly similar to the older Syrian Orthodox tradition that is still practiced in churches across the Middle East. Those churches still have no pews, like it is in Mosques. The architecture of the earliest minarets, which are square rather than round, unquestionably matches the church towers of Byzantine Syria. The Sufi Muslim tradition carried on directly from the point that the Christian Desert Fathers left off. The Ramadan—at first sight one of the most foreign and alienating of Islamic practices—is in fact an an Islamic version of Lent, which in many Eastern Christian churches still involves a strenuous all-day fast.

---

[261] Belloc, Hilaire. *The Great Heresies*, chapter 4.
[262] Fountain of Knowledge, Book II ("On Heresies"), 101.

Besides, Islam contains several of the heresies we discuss in this book. Jesus was born to Mary by divine help, did wondrous deeds, and preached the coming of the prophet Muhammad [Sura 61:6]. He was not crucified, but only appeared to be crucified, and then was taken up to heaven by Allah [Sura 4:157-8]. The doctrine of the "Trinity" is considered one of the worst blasphemies against the unity of Allah. This Christian doctrine, as interpreted in the Qur'an, concerns a divine trinity of Allah, Jesus, and Mary [Sura 5:116], although—in Muslim eyes—Jesus denied that he was divine. To believe that Allah had a son is polytheism according to the Qur'an [Sura 4:171, 5:75, 9:30]. So one could very well make the case that Islam is not a new religion but rather a collection of old heresies. Islam came after Christianity in time and then corrected Christianity's perceived errors like it had been done in older heresies.

The Council of Nicaea would ultimately express its definitive answer to all such heresies, especially Arianism, leading up to the Nicene Creed. The decisive steps towards this answer were taken by the Church Fathers of the 6th and 7th generation.

c. Defenders of the Faith

Athanasius of Alexandria (295-373)

The records tell us that Alexander called upon his brilliant young disciple Athanasius to take over his see as Patriarch of Alexandria once his own energy had gone. The 7th generation was ready to take over the torch in the apostolic succession.

In his *Ecclesiastical History*, which begins with the rise of Arianism and closes with the death of Emperor Theodore in 429, Church historian Theodoret says about Athanasius,

> *Alexander, that admirable bishop, who had successfully withstood the blasphemies of Arius, died five months after the council of Nicaea, and was succeeded in the episcopate of the church of Alexandria by Athanasius. Trained from his youth in sacred studies, Athanasius had attracted general admiration in each ecclesiastical office that he filled. He had, at the general council, so defended the doctrines of the apostles, that while he won the approbation of all the champions of the truth, its opponents learned to look on their antagonist as a personal foe and public enemy.*[263]

Athanasius was certainly not impressive, with his short, delicate stature. Later, the hostile Emperor Julian, better known as "Julian the Apostate," would call him a "black dwarf." But where the ancient, orthodox Faith was concerned, he was obstinate, intransigent, and stubborn as a donkey. After Athanasius had left the desert and became secretary to Alexander, the patriarch of Alexandria, he brought with him a book that he had written—*On the Incarnation*—that would now be officially published. C. S. Lewis would later praise it for the "classical simplicity" of its style. The book is addressed to a recent convert named Macarius, who had heard some confusing objections made against the deity of Christ, probably of Arian origin. It contains many jewels of orthodox Christian doctrine.

In this book, Athanasius made it crystal clear that Jesus was truly God and truly man, both Son of God and Son of man. He came down from Heaven, God from God, light from light, taking on a human form to become our Savior. In his own words:

---

[263] *Ecclesiastical History* 1:25.

> *He took pity on our race, and had mercy on our infirmity, and condescended to our corruption, and, unable to bear that death should have the mastery—lest the creature should perish, and His Father's handiwork in men be spent for nought— He takes unto Himself a body, and that of no different sort from ours.*[264]

Then he stresses that Jesus' death was a necessary condition for our salvation:

> *For the Word, perceiving that no otherwise could the corruption of men be undone save by death as a necessary condition, while it was impossible for the Word to suffer death, being immortal, and Son of the Father; to this end He takes to Himself a body capable of death, that it, by partaking of the Word Who is above all, might be worthy to die in the stead of all, and might, because of the Word which had come to dwell in it, remain incorruptible, and that thenceforth corruption might be stayed from all by the Grace of the Resurrection.*[265]

> *Whence the Word of God came in His own person, that, as He was the Image of the Father, He might be able to create afresh the man after the image. But, again, it could not else have taken place had not death and corruption been done away. Whence He took, in natural fitness, a mortal body, that while death might in it be once for all done away, men made after His Image might once more be renewed. None other then was sufficient for this need, save the Image of the Father.*[266]

---

[264] On the Incarnation 8:2.
[265] Ibid. 9:1.
[266] Ibid. 13:7-9.

He was made man that we might be made God; and He manifested Himself by a body that we might receive the idea of the unseen Father; and He endured the insolence of men that we might inherit immortality. For while He Himself was in no way injured, being impossible and incorruptible and very Word and God, men who were suffering, and for whose sakes He endured all this, He maintained and preserved in His own impassibility.[267]

He that was made manifest and suffered in the body was not man merely, but the Son of God and Saviour of all. For the sun hid His face, and the earth quaked and the mountains were rent: all men were awed. Now these things showed that Christ on the Cross was God, while all creation was His slave, and was witnessing by its fear to its Master's presence. Thus, then, God the Word showed Himself to men by His works.[268]

He gives them a share in His own Image, our Lord Jesus Christ, and makes them after His own Image and after His likeness: so that by such grace perceiving the Image, that is, the Word of the Father, they may be able through Him to get an idea of the Father, and knowing their Maker, live the happy and truly blessed life.[269]

These are only a few passages from his masterpiece *On the Incarnation*, just to show how sound and clear Athanasius' teachings are, and how much they were in defiance of Arianism. In his letters, he was even more explicit about the errors of Arianism. Athanasius saw clearly that the deity of

---

[267] Ibid. 54:3.
[268] Ibid. 19.
[269] Ibid. 63:3.

Christ is actually the cornerstone of our salvation. If Christ were only a creature, the Gospel would not truly be such good news after all. Creation can only be renewed by its Creator. He made this very clear in a passage like this:

> *We do not worship a creature. Far be the thought. For such an error belongs to heathens and Arians. But we worship the Lord of Creation, Incarnate, the Word of God. For if the flesh also is in itself a part of the created world, yet it has become God's body. And we neither divide the body, being such, from the Word, and worship it by itself, nor when we wish to worship the Word do we set Him far apart from the Flesh, but knowing, as we said above, that 'the Word was made flesh,' we recognise Him as God also, after having come in the flesh.*[270]

The question still remained for many Christians how God, the eternal and immortal one, could ever get involved with human flesh. Did the flesh of the Son of man deprive him from his divinity as the Son of God? Athanasius worked very hard to deny this old fallacy:

> *For the Flesh did not diminish the glory of the Word; far be the thought: on the contrary, it was glorified by Him. Nor, because the Son that was in the form of God took upon Him the form of a servant was He deprived of His Godhead. On the contrary, He is thus become the Deliverer of all flesh and of all creation. And if God sent His Son brought forth from a woman, the fact causes us no shame but contrariwise glory and great grace. For He has become Man, that He might deify us in Himself, and He has been born of a woman, and begotten of a Virgin, in order to*

---

[270] Letters 60:3.

transfer to Himself our erring generation.[271]

Obviously, in all his writings, Athanasius was a staunch defender of the orthodoxy of the Church based on apostolic succession. But the crowning glory of his work was the moment when Emperor Constantine had been convinced to summon an assembly of bishops in order to resolve the dispute with Arius in the city of Nicaea. Constantine had invited all 1,800 bishops of the Christian Church within the Roman Empire (about 1,000 in the east and 800 in the west), but a smaller and unknown number attended. Eusebius of Caesarea counted more than 250, Athanasius of Alexandria counted 318, and Eustathius of Antioch estimated some 270 bishops.

Several bishops at the Council of Nicaea had brought along personal assistants. One of them was Athanasius; as a deacon, he accompanied Alexander of Alexandria whom he would succeed later as patriarch of Alexandria. Dorothy Sayers, in her dramatized, but historically correct, 1951 play *The Emperor Constantine*, has Athanasius address the bishops at Nicaea in response to Arius as follows:

> *Beloved Fathers, in whom will you believe? In the Christ of Arius, who is neither true man to bear our sorrows not true God to forgive us our sins? Or in him who, being in the form of God, clung not to his equality with God, but was made in the likeness of man and became obedient unto death for our sakes?*[272]

Athanasius became a champion of the Nicene cause. He was a tireless defender of Trinitarianism and an unwavering foe of the Arians. For good reason, he became known as

---

[271] Ibid. 60:4.
[272] Grand Rapids, MI: Eerdmans Publishing, 1976), 148.

"Athanasius against the World" [*Athanasius contra Mundum*]. In the Eastern Orthodox Church, he is labeled as the "Father of Orthodoxy." Some Protestant groups label him as "Father of the Canon."

Needless to say that Athanasius left quite a mark on the outcome of the Nicene Council. Its Nicene Creed was concluded with the following clause, which sounds very "Athanasian":

> *But those who say: 'There was a time when he was not;' and 'He was not before he was made;' and 'He was made out of nothing,' or 'He is of another substance' or 'essence,' or 'The Son of God is created,' or 'changeable,' or 'alterable'—they are condemned by the holy catholic and apostolic Church.*

Even when the Nicene Council had ended, the fight was far from over for Athanasius. After Nicaea, emperors—both Constantine and his successors—would periodically recant their support for Christian orthodoxy and go back and forth in their official support for Arianism. One could easily say that Arianism was most of the time a state-sponsored heresy. Yet, each time they enforced Arianism again, the emperors had Athanasius battling against them. His opposition to Arianism caused him to be expelled from his see five times, but he regained it each time. After long years of fight and flight, he was restored to his see in Alexandria, where he spent seven peaceful years until his death in 373.

Basil of Caesarea (330-379)

The three Cappadocian Church Fathers—as Basil and the two Gregory's are collective called—would begin to unearth the deeper significance of the Nicene formularies. Of these three Fathers, Basil usually appears as "the doer," Gregory of

Nazianzus as "the dreamer," and Gregory of Nyssa as "the thinker."

Many questions had remained after the Nicaean Council, especially in the minds of Arians. If Jesus, called the Son of God, is also God himself, how can he also be his own son? Besides, what son is as old as his own father? If he is Son, doesn't that mean there was a time he was not the son yet? Many puzzling questions. How could Christians say all of this, let alone make sense of it, without becoming Arians?

Christ reminds us that he and the Father are one.[273] Yet in the Trinity, the Father is not the Son; the Son is not the Father, and the Spirit is neither Father nor Son. They are all "one" precisely by not being each other—one in being, diverse in person. The classic formula, since Tertullian, had been "one substance, three persons." Basil of Caesarea, also called Basil the Great, realized, though, this sounded correct in Latin but did not easily translate into Greek. The Greek word for "person," *prosopon,* was derived from the word for mask worn by actors on the stage, which could easily be understood in terms of Modalism (see 7.b). Hence Basil would rather speak of three *hypostases* instead of three "persons," because the former term conveyed a clearer sense of individuality.

However, the word *hypostasis* used for "being" or "substance" could easily be taken as a synonym for the Greek word *ousia.* So Basil tried to create terminological clarity by distinguishing *ousia*—referring to the one being or nature of God—from *hypostasis*—referring to the way Father, Son, and Holy Spirit participate in that one divine nature. So Tertullian's Trinitarian formula of "one substance, three

---

[273] John 10:30.

persons" was for Basil "one *ousia*, three *hypostases*." This translation became a vital strategy in the war against Arianism.

There still remained one important question about the "three hypostases" or "three persons." If the Father is divine, then Jesus is divine (except for Arians), but what about the Holy Spirit? Basil confronted the problem head-on in his treatise *On the Holy Spirit*. He declared that Scripture does *implicitly* teach the divinity of the Holy Spirit without *explicitly* using the words "the Holy Spirit is God":

> *He existed; He pre-existed; He co-existed with the Father and the Son before the ages. It follows that, even if you can conceive of anything beyond the ages, you will find the Spirit yet further above and beyond. And if you think of the creation, the powers of the heavens were established by the Spirit, the establishment being understood to refer to disability to fall away from good. For it is from the Spirit that the powers derive their close relationship to God, their inability to change to evil, and their continuance in blessedness. Is it Christ's advent? The Spirit is forerunner. Is there the incarnate presence? The Spirit is inseparable. Working of miracles, and gifts of healing are through the Holy Spirit. Demons were driven out by the Spirit of God. The devil was brought to naught by the presence of the Spirit. Remission of sins was by the gift of the Spirit.*[274]

The Holy Spirit had always been mentioned, as early as the apostles and the earliest Church Fathers, but the position of the Holy Spirit in the Trinity had not received much attention yet—that is, until Basil:

---

[274] De Spiritu Sancto 19:49.

And as the Son is glorified of the Father when He says 'I have both glorified it and will glorify it again,' so is the Spirit glorified through His communion with both Father and Son, and through the testimony of the Only-begotten when He says 'All manner of sin and blasphemy shall be forgiven unto men: but the blasphemy against the Holy Ghost shall not be forgiven unto men.'[275]

We are compelled to advance in our conceptions to the highest, and to think of an intelligent essence, in power infinite, in magnitude unlimited, unmeasured by times or ages, generous of Its good gifts, to whom turn all things needing sanctification, after whom reach all things that live in virtue, as being watered by Its inspiration and helped on toward their natural and proper end; perfecting all other things, but Itself in nothing lacking; living not as needing restoration, but as Supplier of life; not growing by additions; but straightway full, self-established, omnipresent, origin of sanctification, light perceptible to the mind, supplying, as it were, through Itself, illumination to every faculty in the search for truth.[276]

How could the importance of the Holy Spirit remain somewhat neglected for such a long time? Indeed, not too many documents of the Church had explicitly dealt with this issue. Basil explains why:

Of the beliefs and practices whether generally accepted or publicly enjoined which are preserved in the Church some we possess derived from written teaching; others we have received delivered to us in a mystery by the tradition of the apostles; and both of these in relation to true

---

[275] Ibid. 46.
[276] Ibid. 22.

> *religion have the same force. ... For were we to attempt to reject such customs as have no written authority, on the ground that the importance they possess is small, we should unintentionally injure the Gospel in its very vitals; or, rather, should make our public definition a mere phrase and nothing more. For instance, to take the first and most general example, who is thence who has taught us in writing to sign with the sign of the cross those who have trusted in the name of our Lord Jesus Christ? What writing has taught us to turn to the East at the prayer? Which of the saints has left us in writing the words of the invocation at the displaying of the bread of the Eucharist and the cup of blessing?*[277]

Apparently, not everything in the Christian Faith has been written down in Scripture. Basil explains this further by making a distinction between written doctrines (*Dogma*) and unwritten traditions (*Kerygma*):

> *For we are not, as is well known, content with what the apostle or the Gospel has recorded, but both in preface and conclusion we add other words as being of great importance to the validity of the ministry, and these we derive from unwritten teaching. ... This is the reason for our tradition of unwritten precepts and practices, that the knowledge of our dogmas may not become neglected and contemned by the multitude through familiarity. Dogma and* Kerugma *are two distinct things; the former is observed in silence; the latter is proclaimed to all the world.*[278]

As we will see later, Basil's teaching, especially about the Holy Spirit, laid the groundwork for the anti-Arian decisions

---
[277] Ibid. 66.
[278] Ibid. 66.

of the next Council, the Council of Constantinople in 381, two years after his death. From his deathbed, Basil had mentioned the qualifications of Gregory of Nazianzus, and had most likely recommended his friend as a champion for the Trinitarian cause in Constantinople. And so he would.

Gregory of Nazianzus (330-390)

The second one of the three Cappadocians, the "dreamer," is Gregory of Nazianzus (or Nazianzen). At a young age, he was sent to a famous school at Caesarea, where he began a friendship with Basil of Caesarea, which deeply affected both their lives, as well as the development of the theology of their age.

Ill-suited for chancery politics, Gregory reluctantly accepted to become Archbishop of Constantinople. A few times he withdrew to monastic seclusion but he was called back to his orthodox minority in the Church of Constantinople, beleaguered by an Arian majority.

The new emperor of the East, Theodosius, had developed a hatred for Arianism and he was the one who would call for the Second Ecumenical Council, that of Constantinople, which met in 381. The Church historian Sozomen (c. 400 - 450) tells us in his *Ecclesial History* about Theodosius,

> *He enacted that the title of Catholic Church should be exclusively confined to those who rendered equal homage to the Three Persons of the Trinity, and that those individuals who entertained opposite opinions should be treated as heretics, regarded with contempt, and delivered over to punishment.*[279]

What Constantine had still done carefully and hesitantly,

---

[279] Ecclesial History 7:4.

Theodosius would do much more directly: interfering with Church issues and doctrines. He would also announce that Gregory should now be enthroned as bishop of Constantinople. During his time in Constantinople, Gregory would dedicate much of his thinking, praying, and writing to the "cause" of the Holy Spirit. He also addressed again the question why the divinity of the Holy Spirit was discovered so late:

> *The Old Testament proclaimed the Father openly, and the Son more obscurely. The New manifested the Son, and suggested the Deity of the Spirit. Now the Spirit Himself dwells among us, and supplies us with a clearer demonstration of Himself. For it was not safe, when the Godhead of the Father was not yet acknowledged, plainly to proclaim the Son; nor when that of the Son was not yet received to burden us further (if I may use so bold an expression) with the Holy Ghost; lest perhaps people might, like men loaded with food beyond their strength, and presenting eyes as yet too weak to bear it to the sun's light, risk the loss even of that which was within the reach of their powers; but that by gradual additions, and, as David says, Goings up, and advances and progress from glory to glory, the Light of the Trinity might shine upon the more illuminated. For this reason it was, I think, that He gradually came to dwell in the Disciples, measuring Himself out to them according to their capacity to receive Him, at the beginning of the Gospel, after the Passion, after the Ascension, making perfect their powers, being breathed upon them, and appearing in fiery tongues. And indeed it is little by little that He is declared by Jesus, as you will learn for yourself if you will read more*

carefully.[280]

Given the unity of the three Persons in the Trinity, says Gregory, we must realize that those who place one Person of the Trinity above another diminish and insult all three:

> [T]he Father is exalted, and the Son is held to be equal to Him, and the Holy Ghost is glorified with Them: we who are of one soul, who mind the same thing, who in nothing injure the Trinity, neither by preferring One Person above another, nor by cutting off any: as those bad umpires and measurers of the Godhead do, who by magnifying One Person more than is fit, diminish and insult the whole.[281]

Still, their internal relationships require further clarification:

> This is what we mean by Father and Son and Holy Ghost. The Father is the Begetter and the Emitter; without passion of course, and without reference to time, and not in a corporeal manner. The Son is the Begotten, and the Holy Ghost the Emission; for I know not how this could be expressed in terms altogether excluding visible things.[282]

Gregory makes sure that the Arian heresy—which includes that there was a time that the Son was not—cannot creep into Christian orthodoxy by claiming there was also a time the Holy Spirit was not:

> And when did the Father come into being. There never was a time when He was not. And the same thing is true of the Son and the Holy Ghost. Ask me again, and again I will answer you,

---

[280] Orations 31:26.
[281] Ibid. 3:6.
[282] Ibid. 29:2, or Third Theological Oration.

> *When was the Son begotten? When the Father was not begotten. And when did the Holy Ghost proceed? When the Son was, not proceeding but, begotten— beyond the sphere of time, and above the grasp of reason; although we cannot set forth that which is above time, if we avoid as we desire any expression which conveys the idea of time.*[283]

Gregory was very aware that a clear and sound theology of the Trinity also calls for a clear and sound Christology:

> *He [Christ] was born— but He had been begotten: He was born of a woman— but she was a Virgin. The first is human, the second Divine. In His Human nature He had no Father, but also in His Divine Nature no Mother. Both these belong to Godhead.*[284]

> *He was baptized as Man— but He remitted sins as God. ... He was tempted as Man, but He conquered as God. ... He lays down His life, but He has power to take it again.*[285]

> *[This] does not mean that the Son has a special will of His own, besides that of the Father, but that He has not; so that the meaning would be, 'not to do Mine own Will, for there is none of Mine apart from, but that which is common to, Me and You; for as We have one Godhead, so We have one Will.'*[286]

Since Arianism claims that the concept of Trinity violates the essence of monotheism—for if God is one then Jesus cannot be God as well—Gregory explains once again what the concept of Trinity really means:

---

[283] Ibid. 29:3, or Third Theological Oration.
[284] Ibid. 29:19, or Third Theological Oration.
[285] Ibid. 29:20, or Third Theological Oration.
[286] Orations 30:12, or Fourth Theological Oration.

> *To us there is One God, for the Godhead is One, and all that proceeds from Him is referred to One, though we believe in Three Persons. For one is not more and another less God; nor is One before and another after; nor are They divided in will or parted in power; nor can you find here any of the qualities of divisible things; but the Godhead is, to speak concisely, undivided in separate Persons; and there is one mingling of Light, as it were of three suns joined to each other.*[287]

If someone objects that the word "Trinity" does not exist in the Scriptures, Gregory tells them that the doctrine of the Faith undergoes a process of development through time, guided by the Holy Ghost, Scripture, Tradition, and the Authority of the Church. Divine Revelation is always progressive in nature—that is, over time, we are granted a fuller and fuller knowledge of God in general, including a fuller understanding of the meaning of prior Revelation. This process of growth resembles the way a river growths—it gets wider and deeper, while remaining the same river:

> *The Old Testament proclaimed the Father openly, and the Son more obscurely. The New manifested the Son, and suggested the Deity of the Spirit. Now the Spirit Himself dwells among us, and supplies us with a clearer demonstration of Himself.*[288]

It is obvious that Gregory played an important role in this process of getting a fuller and fuller understanding of God and what he has revealed to us in Jesus. That's the way the Tradition of the Church works.

---

[287] Ibid. 31:14, or Fifth Theological Oration.
[288] Ibid. 31:26, or Fifth Theological Oration.

Gregory of Nyssa (335-394)

The third one of the three Cappadocians, the "thinker," is Gregory of Nyssa. He was Basil's younger brother and became bishop of Nyssa, in Cappadocia—another hotbed of Arianism.

After the death of Emperor Valens in 378, the new emperor was Theodosius, a steadfast supporter of Nicene orthodoxy. This was good news to those who wished to purge Constantinople of Arian domination. The exiled Nicene party could now gradually return to the city. So it was in this city that the First Council of Constantinople was convened by Emperor Theodosius in 381 for the welfare of religion in that city. It asserted the Faith of Nicaea, and tried to put an end to Arianism in the East. Gregory would be an important participant and would play a key role in this Council's further confirmation of the anti-Arian decrees of the Council of Nicaea.

An important part of Gregory's theology would be to work out the differences between the three Persons of the Trinity based on their *relationships* with each other. He emphasized that the three divine Persons are not independent, separate entities like three human persons would be. Instead, they share in one, single, indivisible divine nature. One nature means one will and one operation. If one of the three Persons wills or acts, all three are simultaneously willing or acting. So although it is only the Son who dies on the Cross, he is never for a moment separated from the Father and the Spirit.

> *We, for instance, confess that the Holy Spirit is of the same rank as the Father and the Son, so that there is no difference between them in anything, to be thought or named, that devotion can ascribe to a Divine nature. We confess that, save His being contemplated as with peculiar*

> *attributes in regard of Person, the Holy Spirit is indeed from God, and of the Christ, according to Scripture, but that, while not to be confounded with the Father in being never originated, nor with the Son in being the Only-begotten, and while to be regarded separately in certain distinctive properties, He has in all else, as I have just said, an exact identity with them.[289]*

As Arians deny the divinity of Jesus, so some other heretics also deny the divinity of the Hole Spirit. Gregory condemns their views:

> *If, then, the Holy Spirit is truly, and not in name only, called Divine both by Scripture and by our Fathers, what ground is left for those who oppose the glory of the Spirit? He is Divine, and absolutely good, and Omnipotent, and wise, and glorious, and eternal; He is everything of this kind that can be named to raise our thoughts to the grandeur of His being.[290]*

Gregory has his opponent proclaim that we have been taught by Scripture that the Father is the Creator, and in the same way that it was "through the Son" that "all things were made." But God's Word tells us nothing of this kind about the Spirit. How, then, can it be right to place the Holy Spirit in a position of equal dignity with One who has displayed such magnificence of power through the Creation? Gregory answers this objection as follows:

> *We are not to think of the Father as ever parted from the Son, nor to look for the Son as separate from the Holy Spirit. As it is impossible to mount to the Father, unless our thoughts are exalted there through the Son, so it is impossible also to*

---

[289] On the Holy Spirit, w/o numbers.
[290] Ibid..

> *say that Jesus is Lord except by the Holy Spirit. Therefore, Father, Son, and Holy Spirit are to be known only in a perfect Trinity, in closest consequence and union with each other, before all creation, before all the ages, before anything whatever of which we can form an idea. The Father is always Father, and in Him the Son, and with the Son the Holy Spirit. If these Persons, then, are inseparate from each other, how great is the folly of these men who undertake to sunder this indivisibility by certain distinctions of time.*[291]

Again, he probes his opponents with some pertinent questions:

> *Well, if He was not present, they must tell us where He was; and whether, while God embraces all things, they can imagine any separate standing-place for the Spirit, so that He could have remained in isolation during the time occupied by the process of creating. If, on the other hand, He was present, how was it that He was inactive? Because He could not, or because He would not, work?*[292]

Here is Gregory's answer:

> *For neither did the Universal God make the universe through the Son, as needing any help, nor does the Only-begotten God work all things by the Holy Spirit, as having a power that comes short of His design; but the fountain of power is the Father, and the power of the Father is the Son, and the spirit of that power is the Holy Spirit; and Creation entirely, in all its visible and spiritual extent, is the finished work of that*

---

[291] Ibid.
[292] Ibid.

> *Divine power. ... we should be justified in calling all that Nature which came into existence by creation a movement of Will, an impulse of Design, a transmission of Power, beginning from the Father, advancing through the Son, and completed in the Holy Spirit.*[293]

> *For how can you confess the Son except by the Holy Spirit? At what moment, then, is the Spirit in a state of separation from the Son, so that when the Father is being worshipped, the worship of the Spirit is not included along with that of the Son?*[294]

The insights of the three Cappadocians left quite an impact on the Council of Constantinople. The Nicene Creed was partly changed and is now sometimes called the Niceno-Constantinopolitan Creed. More particularly, the Creed was expanded with a new section that more explicitly mentioned the Holy Spirit: "We believe in the Holy Spirit, the Lord, the giver of life, who proceeds from the Father (and the Son). With the Father and the Son he is worshipped and glorified. He has spoken through the Prophets. We believe in one holy catholic and apostolic Church. We acknowledge one baptism for the forgiveness of sins. We look for the resurrection of the dead, and the life of the world to come." The part in parentheses is sometimes called "the *filioque* clause." It was first used in Toledo, Spain in 587, and was acknowledged as early as 447 by Pope Leo I in Rome.

The Council of Constantinople was not looked on as an important one at the time; even those present at it seldom refer to it in their writings. Gregory himself, though he assisted at the Council, mentions it only casually in his

---

[293] Ibid.
[294] Ibid.

funeral oration on Meletius of Antioch, who died during the course of this assembly. But nowadays, during most Sunday Masses, the expanded version is said. As a matter of fact, the new Creed was a vital step in the fight against Arianism.

Did the Cappadocians win the battle against Arianism? They did as far as the Catholic Church is concerned. But as it always is the case with heresies, they are hard to eradicate. They live many lives and keep coming back. And Arianism is no exception.

Hilary of Poitiers (300-368)

The previous four defenders of the faith, during the 7th generation, might create the impression that the battle against Arianism was mainly fought in the East. But then we would forget Hilary, the bishop of Poitiers in present-day France. Arianism had made frightful ravages in various regions and threatened to invade Gaul, where it had already mobilized numerous partisans who were more or less secretly affiliated with it. When Emperor Constantius II ordered all the bishops of the West to sign a condemnation of Athanasius, it was the great defender of the Faith in the West, Hilary, who refused to do so, and therefore was banished from France to far off Phrygia. Yet, he would return in full power. Eventually he was called the "Athanasius of the West." He was also called the "Hammer of the Arians."

Only a few years after he bad become bishop of Poitiers, Hilary found himself virtually alone in defending Jesus' deity before a hostile crowd of bishops in the southern French region of Gaul. Those bishops appealed to Emperor Constantius II, who favored a modified version of Arianism and had Hilary exiled from Gaul.

During his exile, Hilary learned everything he could about

what the Arians said and what the orthodox Christians answered and then he began to write. In exile, he wrote his most important work, "On the Trinity" [*De Trinitate*], showing the Bible's consistent witness to the central mystery of Christian faith. Hilary even traveled to Constantinople during his exile, to explain to the city's bishops why their emperor was not orthodox. After the death of Constantius II in 361, Hilary was able to return to his diocese at Poitiers. After being exiled for opposing Arianism in Gaul, he lived to see it squarely condemned in the local church after his return.

To begin with, there was still the old confusion between "begotten" and "created." Hilary cleared the sky. He wrote against heretics:

> *[They] deny that He was born and declare that He was merely created. Birth, they hold, would confess Him to be true God, while creation proves His Godhead unreal; and though this explanation be a fraud against the faith in the unity of God, regarded as an accurate definition, yet they think it may pass muster as figurative language. They degrade, in name and in belief, His true birth to the level of a creation, to cut Him off from the Divine unity, that, as a creature called into being, He may not claim the fullness of the Godhead, which is not His by a true birth.*[295]

Hilary had to fight again against the erroneous idea that making Jesus God opens the door for polytheism and other gods:

> *My soul has been burning to answer these insane attacks. I call to mind that the very centre of a*

---

[295] On the Trinity 1:16.

> *saving faith is the belief not merely in God, but in God as a Father; not merely in Christ, but in Christ as the Son of God; in Him, not as a creature, but as God the Creator, born of God. ... Their purpose is to isolate a solitary God at the heart of the faith by making Christ, though mighty, only a creature; because, so they allege, a birth of God widens the believer's faith into a trust in more gods than one. But we, divinely taught to confess neither two Gods nor yet a solitary God, will adduce the evidence of the Gospels and the prophets for our confession of God the Father and God the Son, united, not confounded, in our faith.*[296]

After he discusses what Jesus is *not*, Hilary explains that Jesus is the only-begotten, perfect, eternal Son of the unbegotten, perfect, eternal Father. He defends the doctrine of the Nicene Council:

> *He therefore, the Unbegotten, before time was begot a Son from Himself; not from any pre-existent matter, for all things are through the Son; not from nothing, for the Son is from the Father's self; not by way of childbirth, for in God there is neither change nor void; not as a piece of Himself cut or torn off or stretched out, for God is passionless and bodiless, and only a possible and embodied being could so be treated, and, as the Apostle says, in Christ dwells all the fullness of the Godhead bodily. Incomprehensibly, ineffably, before time or worlds, He begot the Only-begotten from His own unbegotten substance, bestowing through love and power His whole Divinity upon that Birth. Thus He is the Only-begotten, perfect, eternal Son of the unbegotten,*

---

[296] Ibid. 1:17.

perfect, eternal Father.[297]

He also revisits the *homoousios* issue as it was developed in the East by the Church Fathers there. He discusses how that term was introduced as a defense against heresies, but also how it has been misinterpreted and misunderstood. Hilary defends its use, after explaining what it does *not* mean:

> *They say that this term 'of one substance,' in the Greek* homoousion, *is used to mean and express that the Father is the same as the Son; that is, that He extended Himself out of infinity into the Virgin, and took a body from her, and gave to Himself, in the body which He had taken, the name of Son. This is their first lie concerning the* homoousion. *Their next lie is that this word* homoousion *implies that Father and Son participate in something antecedent to Either and distinct from Both, and that a certain imaginary substance, or* ousia, *anterior to all matter whatsoever, has existed heretofore and been divided and wholly distributed between the Two; which proves, they say, that Each of the Two is of a nature pro-existent to Himself, and Each identical in matter with the Other. And so they profess to condemn the confession of the* homoousion *on the ground that that term does not discriminate between Father and Son, and makes the Father subsequent in time to that matter which He has in common with the Son. And they have devised this third objection to the word* homoousion, *that its meaning, as they explain it, is that the Son derives His origin from a partition of the Father's substance, as though one object had been cut in two and He were the severed portion.*[298]

---

[297] Ibid. 3:3.
[298] Ibid. 4:4.

In contrast, he presents the correct teaching of the Church. He repeats what other Church Fathers had said before him. He shows that in the Godhead there is both Father and Son, and that the Son is both God and man. Therefore, he repeats the orthodox teaching of the Church:

> *She recognises one God, unborn from everlasting; she recognises also one Only-begotten Son of God. She confesses the Father eternal and without beginning; she confesses also that the Son's beginning is from eternity. Not that He has no beginning, but that He is Son of the Father Who has none; not that He is self-originated, but that He is from Him Who is unbegotten from everlasting; born from eternity, receiving, that is, His birth from the eternity of the Father.*[299]

To exclude any misunderstandings, he places the Church's orthodoxy against the heterodoxy of several heretics:

> *We believe that this God gave birth to the Only-begotten Son before all worlds, through Whom He made the world and all things; that He gave birth to Him not in semblance, but in truth, following His own Will, so that He is unchangeable and unalterable, God's perfect creature but not as one of His other creatures, His handiwork, but not as His other works; not, as Valentinus maintained, that the Son is a development of the Father; nor, as Manichæus has declared of the Son, a consubstantial part of the Father; nor, as Sabellius, who makes two out of one, Son and Father at once; nor, as Hieracas, a light from a light, or a lamp with two flames; nor as if He was previously in being and afterwards born or created afresh to be a Son, a*

---

[299] Ibid. 4:6.

notion often condemned by yourself, blessed Pope [Julius I?], publicly in the Church and in the assembly of the brethren.[300]

Simply put, Christians know that Jesus is God but that God is not Jesus. God is one, yet there are not two Gods. We confess neither an isolated God, nor yet two Gods. The Christian paradox cannot be stressed enough:

We have set forth God from God, and at the same time confessed One true God; showing that this presentation of the faith neither falls short of the truth by ascribing singleness of Person to the One true God, nor adds to the faith by asserting the existence of a second Deity. For we confess neither an isolated God, nor yet two Gods. Thus, neither denying that God is One nor maintaining that He is alone, we hold the straight road of truth. Each Divine Person is in the Unity, yet no Person is the One God.[301]

To explain that Jesus is God, but God is not Jesus, Hilary declares that Father and Son are one in name, but they are not two Gods:

[I am engaged] in my warfare against the blasphemous doctrines of modern heresy; that is, in my task of proclaiming that both God the Father and God the Son are God—in other words, that Father and Son are One in name, One in nature, One in the kind of Divinity which they possess—I wished to shield myself from any charge which might be brought against me, either as an advocate of two Gods or of one lonely and isolated Deity. For in God the Father and God the Son, as I have set them forth, no

---

[300] Ibid. 4:12.
[301] Ibid. 7:2.

> *confusion of Persons can be detected; nor in my exposition of Their common nature can any difference between the Godhead of the One and of the Other be discerned.*[302]

Then he analyzes what the Biblical expression "I and the Father are One" means:

> *[T]he words, I and the Father are One, were spoken with regard to the nature which is His by birth. The Jews had rebuked Him because by these words He, being a man, made Himself God. The course of His answer proves that, in this I and the Father are One, He did profess Himself the Son of God, first in name, then in nature, and lastly by birth. For I and Father are the names of substantive Beings; One is a declaration of Their nature, namely, that it is essentially the same in Both; are forbids us to confound Them together; are one, while forbidding confusion, teaches that the unity of the Two is the result of a birth.*[303]

Put differently, Father and Son are One God, but not One Person:

> *For the Father is seen in the Son, and this could be the case neither if He were a lonely Being, nor yet if He were unlike the Son. It is through the Son that the Father is seen: and this mystery which the Son reveals is that They are One God, but not one Person. What other meaning can you attach to this saying of the Lord's, 'He that has seen Me has seen the Father also'? This is no case of identity; the use of the conjunction also shows that the Father is named in addition to the Son. These words, 'The Father also,' are incompatible with the notion of an isolated and single Person.*

---

[302] Ibid. 7:8.
[303] Ibid. 7:25.

> *No conclusion is possible but that the Father was made visible through the Son, because They are One and are alike in nature.*[304]

Heretics often quote the Bible verse where Jesus says about himself, "The Father is greater than I," as proof that the Son is not divine. But Hilary explains how to understand this verse. Jesus uses this verse in reference to his humanity, not his divinity. He prays as man, he obeys as man, and he suffers as man. The form of God had departed from him, for by emptying himself of it, he had taken the form of a servant. So his *divine* nature had not ceased to be, but had taken upon itself the humility of *human* birth. In his own words,

> *If the Son of God, of Whom these things are true, says, 'The Father is greater than I,' can you be ignorant that the Incarnation for your salvation was an emptying of the form of God, and that the Father, unaffected by this assumption of human conditions, abode in the blessed eternity of His own incorrupt nature without taking our flesh? We confess that the Only-begotten God, while He abode in the form of God, abode in the nature of God, but we do not at once reabsorb into the substance of the divine unity His unity bearing the form of a servant. Nor do we teach that the Father is in the Son, as if He entered into Him bodily; but that the nature which was begotten by the Father of the same kind as His own, possessed by nature the nature which begot it: and that this nature, abiding in the form of the nature which begot it, took the form of human nature and weakness. Christ possessed all that was proper to His nature: but the form of God had departed from Him, for by emptying Himself of it, He had taken the form of a servant. The*

---

[304] Ibid. 7:38.

> *divine nature had not ceased to be, but still abiding in Him, it had taken upon itself the humility of earthly birth, and was exercising its proper power in the fashion of the humility it assumed.*[305]

So it is indeed true, in a certain sense, that "The Father is greater than the Son":

> *[F]or manifestly He is greater, Who makes another to be all that He Himself is, Who imparts to the Son by the mystery of the birth the image of His own unbegotten nature, Who begets Him from Himself into His own form, and restores Him again from the form of a servant to the form of God, Whose work it is that Christ, born God according to the Spirit in the glory of the Father, but now Jesus Christ dead in the flesh, should be once more God in the glory of the Father. When, therefore, Christ says that He is going to the Father, He reveals the reason why they should rejoice if they loved Him, because the Father is greater than He.*[306]

Heretics such as Arians also claim that Jesus was not God because "of that day and hour no one knows, neither the angels of heaven, nor the Son, but the Father alone."[307] Hilary is quick to defeat this argument against Jesus' divinity. The *man* in Jesus did not know, but the *God* in him did:

> *We must not therefore think, because He said He did not know the day and the moment, that the Son did not know. As man He wept, and slept, and sorrowed, but God is incapable of tears, or*

---

[305] Ibid. 9:51.
[306] Ibid. 9:54.
[307] Mt. 24:36.

fear, or sleep. According to the weakness of His flesh He shed tears, slept, hungered, thirsted, was weary, and feared, yet without impairing the reality of His Only-begotten nature; equally so must we refer to His human nature, the words that He knew not the day or the hour.[308]

All the above citations are just a small sample of Hilary's numerous efforts to protect the Faith of the Fathers against attacks from Arians and other heretics. His work, like all the work done by other Church Fathers of his generation, has shaped the Faith of the Catholic Church enormously. Their efforts kept the Faith pure in times of serious trouble within the Christian community.

---

[308] On the Trinity 9:75.

9. The 8th Generation (380-430)

a. Backdrop

The 8th generation of Church Fathers grew up in a world where persecution was no longer a threat, because the Roman Empire had more or less "accepted" Christianity—orthodox or unorthodox—as a reality. However, peace brought a new set of issues for the Church. How would the Church deal with the empire? What role should the empire play in Christianity? What authority should the emperor have in doctrinal disputes? In other words, how would the Church handle the relationship between "state" and "religion," between the "throne" and the "altar"?

One view, especially prevalent in the East, practically identified the throne with the altar. This would allow emperors to appoint and remove bishops, with the bishops tacitly concurring. Another view, more prevalent in the West, made a strict distinction between what is Caesar's and what is God's. The latter view was strongly promoted by bishop Ambrose of Milan, who insisted upon the Church's autonomy in religious matters. As he said during one of his famous sermons, "the Emperor is within the Church, not above it."[309]

But there was another side of the coin. The Roman Empire itself, once the most impressive power in history, was in a

---

[309] Sermon Against Auxentius 36.

slow process of falling apart: barbarians were threatening its borders, Huns were at Rome's gates, the military was in disarray, rebellion was rising in the provinces, and the size of the empire had become unwieldy. This caused a new additional problem for the Church: how to deal with more and more "barbarian" peoples, how to salvage Christian doctrine and learning, and how to preserve civil and moral order in the midst of emerging anarchy.

Then there was the problem of the aftermath of Nicaea and the heresy of Arianism. What the previous generation of Church Fathers had gained, culminating in the Council of Nicaea, would almost disappear again when Nicaea came under attack. In this destructive process, the Roman Emperors played a pivotal role—to begin with Constantine himself.

There are many myths surrounding the life of Constantine. Never did he make Christianity the official religion of the empire—Theodosius would, forty years later. Never did he himself become Christian, until just before his death, when he was baptized by an Arian bishop. Neither was he the first emperor to legalize Christianity—that was Gallerius. All he did was using Christianity as a model for unity and stability in his empire. Yet, he was very "generous" to the Church, even to the point of being "dedicated" to the Church. When he discovered at the opening of the Council of Nicaea that some bishops had their right eye torn out, and that they had undergone this mutilation for the sake of religion, he placed his lips upon their wounds, believing that he would extract a blessing from the kiss.

According to the *Ecclesiastical History* of Theodoret, which begins with the rise of Arianism and closes with the death of Theodore in 429, Constantine did the following nice things

The First Christians: Keeping the Faith in Times of Trouble

for the Church:

> *[T]he Church henceforward began to enjoy a settled calm. This was established for her by Constantine, a prince deserving of all praise, whose calling, like that of the divine Apostle, was not of men, nor by man, but from heaven. He enacted laws prohibiting sacrifices to idols, and commanding churches to be erected. He appointed Christians to be governors of the provinces, ordering honour to be shown to the priests, and threatening with death those who dared to insult them. By some the churches which had been destroyed were rebuilt; others erected new ones still more spacious and magnificent. Hence, for us, all was joy and gladness, while our enemies were overwhelmed with gloom and despair.*[310]

So when the unity and the stability of the Church had come under attack by Arianism, Constantine did not quite know what to do. Not being a Christian himself made him blind for what was wrong with Arianism. He had let the Church herself decide by calling for a council, the Council of Nicaea, with the yearning desire of maintaining unanimity among her members. But, for unclear reasons, three years after the Council of Nicaea, Constantine decided to restore Arian bishops to their sees. The unity of the Church and the empire was at stake. Then, a few years later, Arius was allowed to come back from exile, and Athanasius, who had now succeeded Alexander as the new bishop of Alexandria, was ordered to accept Arius back. Athanasius refused, but it did not matter, because Arius had died in the meantime. That was the end of Arius, but not of Arianism.

What had changed Constantine's mind? We don't really

---

[310] Ecclesiastical History 1:1.

know. Perhaps the best explanation is that Arianism is much easier to understand and sell to citizens of the empire than the mystery and paradoxes of the Holy Trinity. Constantine preferred a Church that would absorb almost everyone in the empire. Instead, the Church had shown in Nicaea that she was unwilling to let this happen. Hence, in his eyes, the Church had to change, become more inclusive—that is, Arian—and tolerate heterodoxy. Besides, Constantine was experiencing sudden domestic troubles. At that point the Empress Constantia, Constantine's sister, comes into the picture. She had in her household a confidant, an Arian priest, who kept bombarding her with Arian thoughts. This priest would write his own creed, deceivingly similar to the Nicene Creed, but with one small, hardly noticeable change: *homoiousios* (of a similar substance) instead of *homoousios* (of the same substance)—the difference was in the detail of a small "iota" [*i*]. Whether Constantine noticed this trick or not, we will probably never know.

After Constantine had died in 337, Arians were able to convince his successor in the East, Constantius, that the unity of the empire was best served by a creed that was more "inclusive" than the Nicene Creed. One of the attempts was replacing the term *homoousios* with *homoiousios*. To change the creed "one iota" was to guard against Modalism, but to create an opening for Arianism: the Son is *like* the Father. Almost every bishop was either tricked or forced into signing the new creed. The 8th generation Church Father Jerome would later describe this with the words, "the whole world groaned and was astonished to find itself Arian."

Had Arianism finally prevailed? Certainly not in the Church. Although emperors during the following decades kept oscillating between the Nicaean and Arian camp, the eventual outcome was Nicaean, thanks to the writings of

The First Christians: Keeping the Faith in Times of Trouble

Athanasius and the ones who had followed in his footsteps—Basil the Great, the two Gregorys, and Hilary (see 8.c). More and more bishops would sign on to the Nicene Creed. When the last Arian emperor had died in 378, the new emperor for the East, Theodosius, restored all Church property to those confessing the faith of Nicaea and replaced the Arian bishop of Constantinople with Gregory of Nazianzus again. But Theodosius also recognized the damage Arianism had done to the Church, so he convened another Council in Constantinople to reaffirm the Nicaean Creed.

Besides, Arianism was not over yet in the Western part of the empire. The West had to deal with barbarians (Goths and Huns) at its northern frontier. Many of the Gothic barbarians had been converted to Christianity by Arian missionaries sent from Constantinople. That's why Ambrose, the bishop of Milan and mentor of the young Augustine, had to deal with Arianism in Milan. When the empress Justina of the West ordered him to hand over churches for Arian use, Ambrose refused. Soon barbarian hordes of Arian faith, who would appropriately be known as Vandals, would overrun Italy and Northern Africa, leaving a path of destruction behind and a trail of heresy.

b. Trouble Within: Donatism | Pelagianism

After all the persecutions of Christians that had taken place, the Church had to keep facing the question of how to deal with those who had been "traitors" and wanted to come back into the Church once the persecutions were over. Who should be considered "traitors"? Only those who had offered the required sacrifices to the gods? Or also those who had handed over the Scriptures to the police? Or even those who had handed over only writings that were heretical or not even religious at all?

The issue of "lapsed" Christians was certainly not new. Novatianism had launched similar views earlier (see 6.b). But in the fourth and fifth centuries, the policy of the Novatianists regarding the treatment of the lapsed was inherited by Donatists of North Africa. Donatism was an indirect outcome of Diocletian's severe persecutions. In 303, Diocletian had started the "Great Persecution," the final and fiercest of the ten persecutions through which the early Church had to pass. The governor of the Africa province had been lenient towards the large Christian minority under his rule during the persecutions. He was satisfied when Christians handed over their Scriptures as a token of renouncing their faith. Some Christians acceded to this convenient action. When the persecutions came to an end, however, their critics branded them *traditores*, "those who handed [the holy things] over."

And what about the bishops and priests who were "traitors" themselves or had been ordained by "traitors"? Were their sacraments really valid? Were they validly baptized, let alone ordained? A clear and rigorous answer came from Donatism. It considered holiness a personal property of the minister of sacraments, whether bishop or priest. If the minister was a sinner, then he could not possibly administer God's grace. Hence, Donatists considered themselves the only true and holy Church that had kept itself clean and truthful during the persecutions. All other Christians were part of an "anti-church" that had polluted herself with treason, the way Judas Iskariot had. Thus the true Church had been reduced to the little sect of Donatists, especially so in Northern Africa. It had inherited the rigorism of the earlier Montanists (see 5.b).

The Church rejected this kind of rigorism as a schismatic heresy. She was given the power by Jesus to forgive sins,

The First Christians: Keeping the Faith in Times of Trouble

even serious sins. And she can use this power, not because the minister is sinless but because the minister was given this power by Jesus himself. As Rob Bennett said about popes, "the pope has never been held by the Church to be *impeccable* (incapable of sin) but only *infallible* (incapable of error)."[311] The legendary novelist Flannery O'Connor once said, "Christ never said that the Church would be operated in a sinless or intelligent way, but that it would not teach error."[312]

Basically at the same time that Donatism was emerging, another heresy stirred up the Christian community: Pelagianism. It is the belief that original sin did not taint human nature and that we are born with the same purity and moral abilities as Adam was when he was first made by God. This theological theory is named after the British monk Pelagius (c. 360 – 418), who asserted a strong version of the doctrine of free will. Pelagianism has come to be identified with the view that human beings can earn salvation by their own efforts—they determine their own destiny. To put this in a catchphrase: God helps those who help themselves.

Pelagius left his native land sometime around the year 400 and journeyed first to Italy, then to Africa, and finally went to the Holy Land. Wherever he landed, Catholics became suspicious of his teachings, but he usually was clever enough to escape detection. He even deceived the great Church Father Augustine, at least for a while. When he reached the Holy Land, he first won to his doctrine its weak bishop, John of Jerusalem. Although he had to appear before a synod of fourteen bishops in the city of Diospolis, currently called Lod

---

[311] Four Witnesses, 290.
[312] Flannery O'Connor, *The Habit of Being* (New York: Vintage, 1979), p. 30.

southeast of Tel Aviv, he managed to escape condemnation.

Pelagius had been disturbed by the immorality he encountered in Rome where he saw Christians using human frailty as an excuse for their failure to live a Christian life. In response, he taught that the human will, as created with its abilities by God, was sufficient to live a sinless life (although he did believe that God's grace assisted every good work). In other words, Pelagius defended complete self-determination—changing your will merely by an act of will. It has been argued that Pelagius' ideas were chiefly rooted in the pagan philosophy of Naturalism in the sense that it exalts nature and depreciates the supernatural order—the order of grace. This may remind us of the "blank slate" view of Jean-Jacques Rousseau in the 18th century: a child is born completely free of any predisposition or vulnerabilities; any wickedness comes from society.

The Pelagians begin by denying original sin. They hold that the sin of Adam harmed only himself. The value of Christ's redemption was, in their view, limited mainly to instruction (*doctrina*) and example (*exemplum*), which God threw into the balance as a counterweight against Adam's wicked example, so that nature retains the ability to conquer sin and to gain eternal life even without the aid of grace. From this follows that babies are born now in identically the same condition in which Adam was before the Fall; unbaptized babies are saved without baptism, and adults can be saved by practicing the natural virtues without Faith or grace.

Many people today who consider themselves to be orthodox Catholics would probably find nothing wrong with these beliefs. Many priests and religious would probably sign these statements, if they did not remember from their history books that they were condemned as heresies. As a matter of fact, at the Council of Ephesus (431)—the third of the Ecumenical Councils, after Nicaea in 325 and Constantinople in 381—Pelagianism was denounced and declared a heresy, because it held that it was possible, at least in theory, to live a morally perfect life without special aid from God. After that condemnation, the heresy would no longer disturb the Church in the East, so that the Greek historians of the fifth century do not even mention neither the heresy nor the name of its founder.

But the heresy continued to smolder in the West and never died out completely. Our modern society is still filled with "Pelagians," who may not even know they are Pelagians. They are solitary individuals navigating on their own towards goals of their own. They believe that we are fully self-made, in full control of our own history and destination. They declare humanity as the measure of all things by pronouncing that all our problems can be entirely solved by using the right human knowledge, technology, reasoning, and judgment. They have no need of God and his redemption and salvation, for there is nothing wrong with us. It is basically the heresy of paganism.

c. Defenders of the Faith

Jerome (347-420)

The Church Father Jerome was born around 342 in a small town in Dalmatia, now part of Croatia, and he died in the year 420 in the town of Bethlehem, where Jesus was born. We notice from the span of his life how close he was to the time of the last persecution. Although persecution was supposed to have ended when Constantine proclaimed the liberty of the Church by the Edict of Milan (313), it actually continued in the East under the pagan emperor Licinius (308-324) for many years after the Edict was issued. During the persecution of Julian the Apostate (361-363), Jerome would have been a young man of about twenty or twenty-one. As a young man, he had become the protégé of Gregory Nazianzus, sat next to Gregory of Nyssa at the Council of Constantinople, and discussed the proceedings with him.

Jerome is probably best known for his translation of the Bible into Latin—the translation that became known as the *Vulgate*. The Old Testament was written in Hebrew, but when more and more Jews in the Diaspora were no longer fluent in Hebrew, a legendary group of seventy Jewish scholars was commissioned in the 3rd century BC to make a Greek translation, commonly known as the *Septuagint* (Greek for "seventy"). The New Testament was mainly written in Greek as well. But when the division between East and West became more pronounced and an increasing number of Christians in the West were no longer fluent in Greek, several individuals had made Latin translations of parts of the Bible. In 382, Pope Damasus I commissioned Jerome to make a new and official Latin translation of the entire Bible.

Jerome was highly qualified for the job. In addition to Latin, he knew Greek and Hebrew well, which makes him extremely competent to undertake such an enormous task of translating the entire Bible. Besides, he was able to base his translation on original manuscripts that have since perished during the persecutions when Christians had to hand over their Bibles to the officials. So he had access to older documents than modern Bible scholars do.

In the 5th century, when Jerome translated the Bible from the original languages into Latin, Latin was the language of the people. His Bible is therefore called the *Vulgate*, the "people's version." But when more and more people in the

The First Christians: Keeping the Faith in Times of Trouble

West were no longer able to read Latin, there was a growing need for translations in the *vernacular*. Although many think that such translations did not exist until the 16th century—until the time of the Reformation, that is—there were some earlier examples. In 7th century Britain, before English was even a language, Caedmon, a monk of Whitby, paraphrased most of the Bible into the common tongue. During the early 8th century, Bede the Venerable also translated parts of the Bible into the language of the common British people. As a matter of fact, prior to Martin Luther's Bible translation in German, there had been over 20 versions of the whole Bible translated into the various German dialects by Catholics. In Italy there were more than 40 editions of the Bible before the first Protestant version appeared, beginning at Venice in 1471; and 25 of these were in the Italian language before 1500, with the explicit permission of Rome.

It is widely unknown that the first book ever printed in the West was not a Protestant but a Catholic Bible, a product of Johann Gutenberg, the inventor of the printing press in Germany. Even the first printed Bible in English was published by British Catholics exiled to France at the colleges of Douay and Rheims. They published the New Testament in 1582 and the Old Testament in 1610. This *Douay-Rheims* Bible was a rather literal translation of Jerome's Latin *Vulgate*, and went through several revisions. It was completed in 1610, one year before the Protestant King James Version (KJV) was published. The Catholic New Testament translation, published in 1582, was actually one of the sources used by the KJV translators. One of the reasons was that Jerome's Latin Vulgate was based on original texts that are no longer available to us. So Jerome remains an invaluable link for Christianity, going back to the very first

Christians.

But Jerome did much more than translating the Bible. He emerged as one of the chief critics of the new heresies emerging at the time — Donatism and Pelagianism.

Let's start very briefly with his battle against Donatism. Jerome rejects the idea of Donatists that bishops or priests should be flawless, for he stresses that no one is without some fault:

> *God certainly wishes bishops or priests to be such as the chosen vessel teaches they should be. As to the first qualification it is seldom or never that one is found without reproach; for who is it that has not some fault, like a mole or a wart on a lovely body? If the Apostle himself says of Peter that he did not tread a straight path in the truth of the Gospel, and was so far to blame that even Barnabas was led away into the same dissimulation, who will be indignant if that is denied to him which the chief of the Apostles had not?*[313]

Jerome also rejects the rigorist part of the Donatists and the idea of an elite Church. The Church is not flawless, neither are here leaders. He sees sin as an unavoidable part of human nature. The problem with Donatism is that no person is morally pure, for we are all sinners—even bishops are:

> *Seldom or never, I say, is there a man who has all the virtues which a bishop should have. And yet if a bishop lacked one or two of the virtues in the list, it does not follow that he can no longer be called righteous, nor will he be condemned for his deficiencies, but will be crowned for what he*

---

[313] Against the Pelagians 1:22.

has.[314]

Jerome also rejects the idea of Donatism that the effectiveness of the sacraments depends on the moral character of the minister. Sacraments do not cease to be effective if the moral character of the minister is in question or is even proven to be faulty. Rather, the sacraments are powerful because of what they are—visible representations of spiritual realities. God is the one who works in and through them; and he is not restricted by the moral state of the administrant:

> *The next point is that the bishop must be free from accusation, that he have a good report from them who are without, that no reproaches of opponents be levelled at him, and that they who dislike his doctrine may be pleased with his life. I suppose it would not be easy to find all this.*[315]

Even much more so than combatting Donatism, Jerome had to wage a life-long battle with the heresy of Pelagianism, which is somehow connected with Donatism, because they both assume that we are completely free to choose good and avoid evil. Pelagians deny original sin, and regard man as by nature morally and spiritually well. In his response to the Pelagian heresy, Jerome proclaims that, by nature, all humans sin:

> *We are not told that a man can be without sin, which is your view, but that God, if He chooses, can keep a man free from sin, and of His mercy guard him so that he may be without blemish. And I say that all things are possible with God; but that everything which a man desires is not possible to him, and especially, an attribute*

---

[314] Ibid. 1:22.
[315] Ibid. 1:22.

which belongs to no created thing you ever read of.[316]

In opposition to Pelagianism, Jerome defends the Catholic Faith in the Redemption achieved by Jesus through his death on the Cross. He argues: if the sin of Adam hurt only himself, how are we then saved by the sufferings and death of Jesus? Pelagianism actually renders vain the Cross of Jesus Christ:

> *And in the Epistle of John, 'If we say that we have no sin, we deceive ourselves, and the truth is not in us.' You, on the other hand, maintain that 'A man can be without sin,' and that you may give your words the semblance of truth, you immediately add, 'And easily keep the commandments of God, if he chooses,' and yet they have been seldom or never kept by any one. Now, if they were easy, they ought to have been kept by all. But if, to concede you a point, at rare intervals some one may be found able to keep them, it is clear that what is rare is difficult. ... You should have known that the Church admits even failures through ignorance and sins of mere thought to be offenses; so much so that she bids sacrifices be offered for errors, and the high priest who makes intercession for the whole people previously offers victims for himself. Now, if he were not himself righteous, he would never be commanded to offer for others. Nor, again, would he offer for himself if he were free from sins of ignorance.*[317]

No one would rise up today with so much indignation to do battle against the Pelagian heresy as Jerome did. He set himself to wage war against the heresy, and together with Augustine—after he had awoken from his deception—

---

[316] Ibid. 1:24.
[317] Ibid. 1:32.

succeeded in having it condemned by a local synod at Carthage in Africa in 418. When Pope Zozimus ratified the acts of the Council, Augustine uttered the famous words, "Rome has spoken, the case is ended" *[Roma locuta est, causa finita est]*. The case was ended indeed as far as the Church was concerned, but not for Jerome, who continued to be harassed to the very end of his life by the Pelagians. He was ultimately punished for his defense of the Catholic Faith, when adherents of Pelagianism burned the monasteries Jerome had founded.

Augustine of Hippo (354-440)

Augustine is probably the most influential theologian in the history of the Western Church and the most-cited Church Father in Church documents, outside the Bible. He is probably best known for his "best-seller" *Confessiones*. But he also dealt death blows to two major heresies: Donatism and Pelagianism.

Augustine considered Donatism a real danger for the Church. First of all, he rejected the sectarian mentality of the Donatists as opposed to the universal and Catholic family of God that Jesus had proclaimed:

> *We must hold to the Christian religion and to communication in her Church, which is catholic and which is called catholic not only by her own members but even by all her enemies. For when heretics or the adherents of schisms talk about her, not among themselves but with strangers, willy-nilly they call her nothing else but Catholic. For they will not be understood unless they distinguish her by this name which the whole world employs in her regard.*[318]

---

[318] The True Religion 7:12.

His other problem with Donatism was its claim that the effectiveness of the sacraments depends on the moral character of the minister. In other words, if a minister involved in a serious enough sin were to baptize a person, that baptism would be considered invalid. Augustine pointed out, as Jerome had done before him, that the problem with Donatism is that no person is morally pure. The effectiveness of the administration of sacraments does not cease to be effective when the sinfulness of the minister is in question. God is the one who works in and through them, and God is not restricted by the moral state of the administrant. The point is that the Church is holy, but her members are not. She is not holy thanks to the people who bear a certain title—instead, it is her message that makes her holy.

Augustine stresses that ministers are not holy on their own account, so when they administer the sacraments, they act on behalf of Christ, who is holy:

> *But he who is a proud minister is reckoned with the devil; but the gift of Christ is not contaminated, which flows through him pure, which passes through him liquid, and comes to the fertile earth. Suppose that he is stony, that he cannot from water rear fruit; even through the stony channel the water passes, the water passes to the garden beds; in the stony channel it causes nothing to grow, but nevertheless it brings much fruit to the gardens. For the spiritual virtue of the sacrament is like the light: both by those who are to be enlightened is it received pure, and if it passes through the impure it is not stained. Let the ministers be by all means righteous, and seek not their own glory, but His glory whose ministers they are; let them not say, The baptism*

is mine; for it is not theirs.[319]

The Church would later formalize this as follows. The sacraments are not really works of the minister at all (*ex opere operantis*) but rather works of Christ, who instituted them and had given them their own intrinsic efficacy (*ex opere operato*), independent of the personal holiness of the minster, or lack thereof. So the minister may lose his own soul through sinfulness, schism, or heresy, but he cannot lose the charisma of his ordination in the process. This explains why converts don't have to be baptized again if they had been baptized in "another" Church—contrary to what Cyprian had once proclaimed (see 6.c).

Not only did Augustine battle Donatism, he also became well known as a strong opponent of Pelagianism. Like all heresies, Pelagianism makes an exclusive choice, in this case between divine grace and human freedom—making it an either-or option. Pelagianism choses human freedom over God's grace, for in its view, defending the power of God's grace would mean a denial of man's free will, the latter of which allegedly had to be defended at all costs.

Augustine does not deny either human freedom or God's grace. On the one hand, he says there must be human freedom: "There is, to begin with, the fact that God's precepts themselves would be of no use to a man unless he had free choice of will, so that by performing them he might obtain the promised rewards."[320] So he does not deny our capacity to make choices. On the other hand, there must also be God's grace, for "the determination of the human will is insufficient, unless the Lord grant it victory in answer to

---

[319] Tractates on the Gospel of John 5:15.
[320] On Grace and Free Will 2.

prayer that it enter not into temptation."[321] So Augustine does not deny that we can make choices, but he does deny that we can make the right choices without God's grace. We were given the freedom to choose, but after the Fall, we tend to choose the wrong things. So it is not our capacity to choose that is corrupted, but for us to make the right choices we do need God's grace.

Pelagianism, on the other hand, does not just deny God's grace, but it says that God's grace is given according to our merits achieved through human freedom. Augustine has a very swift response to this claim: "And so they [Pelagians] labour with all their might to show that God's grace is given according to our merits—in other words, that grace is not grace.[322] So the question remains why we do need God's grace if we have the capacity to make free choices. The answer is that our freedom has been corrupted since the Fall in Paradise.

Paul the Apostle had already described the problem of a corrupted will: "For I do not do the good I want, but I do the evil I do not want. Now if [I] do what I do not want, it is no longer I who do it, but sin that dwells in me."[323] Augustine touches on this issue when he mentions how he stole pears from an orchard as a child:

> *There was a pear-tree close to our vineyard, heavily laden with fruit, which was tempting neither for its colour nor its flavour. To shake and rob this some of us wanton young fellows went, late one night (having, according to our disgraceful habit, prolonged our games in the streets until then), and carried away great loads,*

---

[321] Ibid. 9.
[322] Ibid. 11.
[323] Rom. 7:19-20.

> *not to eat ourselves, but to fling to the very swine, having only eaten some of them; and to do this pleased us all the more because it was not permitted. Behold my heart, O my God; behold my heart, which You had pity upon when in the bottomless pit. Behold, now, let my heart tell You what it was seeking there, that I should be gratuitously wanton, having no inducement to evil but the evil itself. It was foul, and I loved it. I loved to perish. I loved my own error—not that for which I erred, but the error itself.*[324]

This is an example of the corrupted will that chooses evil for its own sake—a consequence of original sin in which the will rebels against reason and becomes a slave at the command of passions. Just as the good can be loved for its own sake, as something intrinsically desired, so evil can be willed for its own sake. That's when Augustine speaks of *Original Sin*: "For through the sin of the first man, which came from his free will, our nature became corrupted and ruined; and nothing but God's grace alone, through Him who is the Mediator between God and men, and our Almighty Physician, succours it."[325] Whereas Pelagians reduced the influence of Adam's fault to bad example, Augustine stresses that it is a sin that has affected all of humanity ever since, making it an *Original Sin*. The original sin did not destroy human freedom but certainly corrupted it.

Augustine's balanced view would later be distorted by the Protestant Reformers. Martin Luther went as far as denying free will in his Heidelberg Thesis: "'Free will' after the fall is nothing but a word, and as long as it is doing what is within it, it is committing deadly sin." And John Calvin declared that the human merit of works would "make void the Cross

---

[324] Confessions 2:4.
[325] On the Grace of Christ, and on Original Sin 2:55.

of Christ." The Catholic Church rejects such extreme positions as the outcome of a false dilemma. She stresses that God's grace and human works are intricately connected. Again we see that heresies choose and pick from what should be connected—in this case, Grace instead of works, or the Fall instead of free will.

In other words, we are born needing salvation. Everyone's will needs to be healed. The human will is not taken away, but changed from bad to good, and assisted when it is good. Somewhere else he says, "Who created you without your cooperation, will not save you without your cooperations."[326] For Augustine, Christian life is a lifelong process of the recovery of freedom—greater and fuller freedom thanks to the grace of God:

> *When God says, 'Turn ye unto me, and I will turn unto you,' one of these clauses—that which invites our return to God—evidently belongs to our will; while the other, which promises His return to us, belongs to His grace. Here, possibly, the Pelagians think they have a justification for their opinion which they so prominently advance, that God's grace is given according to our merits. ... Now the persons who hold this opinion fail to observe that ... our turning to God were itself God's gift.*[327]

This gift of God's grace becomes most prominent in the sacrament of Baptism. Augustine speaks of two births that a man must go through—being born from the womb and being born again in Baptism:

> *[H]is first birth holds a man in that bondage from which nothing but his second birth delivers*

---

[326] Sermon 169, 13.
[327] On Grace and Free Will 10.

> him. The devil holds him, Christ liberates him: Eve's deceiver holds him, Mary's Son frees him: he holds him, who approached the man through the woman; He frees him, who was born of a woman that never approached a man: he holds him, who injected into the woman the cause of lust; He liberates him, who without any lust was conceived in the woman. The former was able to hold all men in his grasp through one; nor does any deliver them out of his power but One, whom he was unable to grasp. The very sacraments indeed of the Church, which she administers with due ceremony, according to the authority of very ancient tradition ... show plainly enough that infants, even when fresh from the womb, are delivered from the bondage of the devil through the grace of Christ.[328]

Because of all of this, Augustine holds, against the Pelagians, that our free will is indeed a reality, but this free will has been so corrupted that it needs to be redeemed and guided and enforced by the grace of God. It is not our human freedom that is corrupt, but it is our will to choose what is good that needs grace. The key point is that we would not need the salvation Jesus made possible for us if human freedom were all that matters:

> Now if faith is simply of free will, and is not given by God, why do we pray for those who will not believe, that they may believe? This it would be absolutely useless to do, unless we believe, with perfect propriety, that Almighty God is able to turn to belief wills that are perverse and opposed to faith.[329]

So when Pelagians claim that God's grace is given according

---

[328] On the Grace of Christ, and on Original Sin 1:45.
[329] On Grace and Free Will 29.

to our merits, because we have freely chosen to follow God's Law and Commandments, Augustine retorts:

> *Grace makes us lovers of the law; but the law itself, without grace, makes us nothing but breakers of the law. ... But it was because they [the apostles] had been chosen, that they chose Him; not because they chose Him that they were chosen.*[330]

This was just a brief summary of how Augustine dealt with the heresies of Donatism and Pelagianism. But in his fight against heresies, he did much more than just telling Christians what *not* to believe; he also and more positively discussed what they *should* believe. He tried to do so by speaking to the "average" Catholic. He did this most extensively in summarizing what the Catholic Church teaches us about the Holy Trinity—a "gold mine" for many heretics, as we have seen in previous chapters. Yet, Augustine is very patient with those former heretics and with those who find difficulty in the Christian Faith, as he expresses here:

> *Some persons, however, find a difficulty in this faith; when they hear that the Father is God, and the Son God, and the Holy Spirit God, and yet that this Trinity is not three Gods, but one God; and they ask how they are to understand this.... They wish to understand how the Trinity uttered that voice which was only of the Father; and how the same Trinity created that flesh in which the Son only was born of the Virgin; and how the very same Trinity itself wrought that form of a dove, in which the Holy Spirit only appeared.*[331]

---

[330] Ibid. 38.
[331] On the Trinity 1:8.

Augustine is a good pastor who had to fight for the truth himself. He realizes how confusing the doctrine of the Trinity can be and how the Church Fathers before him had to struggle with this Mystery:

> *All those Catholic expounders of the divine Scriptures, both Old and New, whom I have been able to read, who have written before me concerning the Trinity, Who is God, have purposed to teach, according to the Scriptures, this doctrine, that the Father, and the Son, and the Holy Spirit intimate a divine unity of one and the same substance in an indivisible equality; and therefore that they are not three Gods, but one God: although the Father has begotten the Son, and so He who is the Father is not the Son; and the Son is begotten by the Father, and so He who is the Son is not the Father; and the Holy Spirit is neither the Father nor the Son, but only the Spirit of the Father and of the Son, Himself also co-equal with the Father and the Son, and pertaining to the unity of the Trinity.*[332]

This has also profound consequences for how we think about Jesus. Augustine stands in a powerful Tradition and merely repeats what Church Fathers before him had taught us:

> *The Son of God, then, is equal to God the Father in nature, but less in 'fashion.' For in the form of a servant which He took He is less than the Father; but in the form of God, in which also He was before He took the form of a servant, He is equal to the Father. In the form of God He is the Word, 'by whom all things are made'; but in the form of a servant He was 'made of a woman, made under the law, to redeem them that were*

---

[332] Ibid. 1:7.

> *under the law.' In like manner, in the form of God He made man; in the form of a servant He was made man.*[333]

Augustine realizes how confusing all of this is, because there is also terminological confusion: Greek Christians speak of "one essence and three substances," but Latin Christians of "one essence or substance with three persons." But Augustine tells us to keep in mind that "essence usually means nothing else than substance in our language, that is, in Latin."[334] He tries sincerely to explain this to non-theologians, for Church doctrine had not made things easier by discussing the intricacies of the Trinitarian doctrine:

> *For certainly, since the Father is a person, and the Son a person, and the Holy Spirit a person, therefore there are three persons: since then the Father is God, and the Son God, and the Holy Spirit God, why not three Gods? Or else, since on account of their ineffable union these three are together one God, why not also one person; so that we could not say three persons, although we call each a person singly, just as we cannot say three Gods, although we call each singly God, whether the Father, or the Son, or the Holy Spirit? Is it because Scripture does not say three Gods? But neither do we find that Scripture anywhere mentions three persons. Or is it because Scripture does not call these three, either three persons or one person (for we read of the person of the Lord, but not of the Lord as a person), that therefore it was lawful through the mere necessity of speaking and reasoning to say three persons, not because Scripture says it, but because Scripture does not contradict it: whereas, if we were to say three Gods, Scripture*

---

[333] Ibid. 1:14.
[334] Ibid. 7:7.

> *would contradict it.*[335]

Yet, the Church has this important task to defend and define what Christians believe and do in their Faith. So Augustine as a late Church Father ties his own Catholic Faith back to previous Church Fathers, and ultimately to Jesus himself:

> *As to those other things which we hold on the authority, not of Scripture, but of tradition, and which are observed throughout the whole world, it may be understood that they are held as approved and instituted either by the apostles themselves, or by plenary Councils, whose authority in the Church is most useful, e.g. the annual commemoration, by special solemnities, of the Lord's passion, resurrection, and ascension, and of the descent of the Holy Spirit from heaven, and whatever else is in like manner observed by the whole Church wherever it has been established.*[336]

What we discussed here about Augustine is only a small part of what he did for the Church. But it is hopefully enough to see why Augustine's influence on Christianity is thought by many to be second only to that of the Apostle Paul. No wonder, theologians, both Catholic and Protestant, look upon him as one of the founders of Western theology. Augustine's adaptation of classical thought to Christian teaching created a theological system of great power and lasting influence. His numerous written works helped lay the foundation for much of medieval and modern Christian thought.

---

[335] Ibid. 7:9.
[336] Letters 54:1:1.

10. The 9th Generation (430-480)

a. Backdrop

The Western part of the Roman Empire was facing big troubles. Early in the 5th century, the barbarians swept from the frontiers to Rome's city gates. Visigoths sacked Rome in 410. In 455, Vandals seized the city. The last emperor of the West died in 476. And Rome descended into anarchy, as did much of Western Europe: the military dissolved, the court system collided, and civil order collapsed. The civilized world of the Roman Empire had been overrun by uncivilized barbarians from outside the Empire.

Only the Church survived in the West as a unified, multinational force for order. Presiding over this social system on a local level was the bishop, but presiding over it all was the pope in Rome. To name just a few gigantic popes during this time of turmoil: Pope Leo the Great (from 440 to 461) and Pope Gregory the Great (from 590 to 604). Let's find out what they did contribute to the Church and to the West.

Not long after his elevation to the Chair of Peter, Pope Leo saw himself compelled to combat energetically the heresies which seriously threatened church unity even in the West. Leo had been informed by Bishop Septimus of Altinum that priests and deacons who had been adherents of Pelagius (see

9.b) had been admitted to communion without an explicit abjuration of their heresy. The pope sharply censured this procedure, and directed that a provincial synod should be assembled, at which such persons were to be required to abjure Pelagianism publicly and to subscribe to an unequivocal confession of Faith—mercy, but not unconditionally.

In Leo's conception of his duties as supreme pastor, the maintenance of strict ecclesiastical discipline occupied a prominent place. This was particularly important at a time when the continual ravages of the barbarians were disrupting all conditions of life, and the rules of morality were being seriously violated. When Northern Italy had been devastated by Attila, Pope Leo personally met with the King of the Huns and prevented him from marching upon Rome. A few years later the Vandal king, Genseric, came from Africa and appeared with his army before the walls of Rome, then almost defenseless. This time Pope Leo was able to win from the invader the promise to restrain his troops from arson and carnage. After ten days of pillaging the city, the Vandals withdrew, taking back to Africa a host of captives and immense booty, but sparing the churches of Saints Peter and Paul.

Pope Leo also felt responsible for what was happening to the Church in the East. A Council had been summoned at Ephesus by Emperor Theodosius to tackle heresies in the East. This gathering, which Leo branded as a "Robber Council," refused to read to the Council a letter from Leo, called the *Tome*. Two years later, in 451, under a new emperor, Marcian, a much larger Council was held at Chalcedon, a city in Asia Minor. At least six hundred bishops were present and Leo's letter could finally be read. "Peter has spoken by the mouth of Leo!" exclaimed the bishops when they heard statements like this:

> *He whom nothing could contain was content to be contained: abiding before all time He began to be in time: the Lord of all things, He obscured His immeasurable majesty and took on Him the form of a servant: being God that cannot suffer, He did not disdain to be man that can, and, immortal as He is, to subject Himself to the laws of death. The Lord assumed His mother's nature without her faultiness: nor in the Lord Jesus Christ, born of the Virgin's womb, does the wonderfulness of His birth make His nature unlike ours. For He who is true God is also true man.*[337]

More than a century later another giant would become pope: Gregory the Great. He is credited with re-energizing the Church's missionary work among the non-Christian peoples of northern Europe. He is most famous for sending a mission, under Augustine of Canterbury, to evangelize the pagan Anglo-Saxons of England. His influence in Britain was such that he is justly called the "Apostle of the English." The mission was so successful that missionaries from England would later set out for other pagan regions: the Netherlands and Germany.

The preaching of the Catholic Faith and the elimination of all deviations from it was a key element during Gregory's pontificate. He made every effort possible to root out paganism in Gaul, Donatism in Africa, and Arianism among the Lombards and Visigoths. Eventually, he would align them with Rome in religion. Besides, the inroads of the Lombards had filled the city of Rome with a multitude of poverty-stricken refugees, for whose support Gregory made

---

[337] in the "Tome," Letter 8:4.

provision, using for this purpose the existing machinery of the ecclesiastical districts, each of which had its deaconry or "office of alms."

Pope Gregory exercised in many respects a momentous influence on the doctrine, the organization, and the discipline of the Catholic Church. To him we must look for an explanation of the religious situation of the Middle Ages. Without him, the evolution of medieval Christianity would be nearly inexplicable. The influence of Gregory the Great is so widespread that the great modern scholar Henri de Lubac dubbed the period from Gregory's death up to the thirteenth century "The Gregorian Middle Ages." Preachers were everywhere citing, referencing, and, generally, re-using the work of one they affectionately called "our Gregory" or "the homilist of the Church." He is also known as "the Great Visionary of Modern Educational System," because of his writings and contribution to the school system of education.

Gregory is also rightly called the father of the medieval papacy. He claimed for the Apostolic See, and for himself as pope, a primacy—not of honor, but of supreme authority over the Church Universal. In the Eastern Churches, too, the papal authority was exercised with a frequency unusual before his time, and we find no less an authority than the Patriarch of Alexandria submitting himself humbly to the pope's "commands." From then on, Rome as the papal capital would continue to be the center of the Christian world.

Gregory also clearly defined how to deal with the imperial government of the East, centered in Constantinople. He looked upon Church and State as co-operating in a united whole, but with two distinct spheres, ecclesiastical and secular. Presiding over this commonwealth were the pope and the emperor, each supreme in his own department. Yet, he often would call in the aid of the secular arm to suppress schism, heresy, or idolatry. On the other hand, when the emperor interfered in Church matters, the pope's policy was to comply if possible, unless obedience was sinful.

b. Trouble Within: Nestorianism

In 428, a man named Nestorius was elevated to be patriarch of Constantinople. He loved the phrase "strictly speaking," and repeated it happily. He rejected, for example, the title for Mary as "Mother of God" [*Theotokos*]—which title had become very popular among Christians. When monks went to Nestorius asking whether "Theotokos" was an appropriate term for Mary, he told them that, "strictly speaking," Mary did not precede God in time the way an ordinary mother precedes an ordinary child. This answer did not satisfy the monks, who later said, "If Mary is not, 'strictly speaking,' the Mother of God [Theotokos], then her son is not, 'strictly speaking,' God!" To which Nestorians retorted: "Let no man call Mary Mother of God for she was but a woman, and it is impossible for God to be born of a woman."

Nestorius thought the title "Mother of God" was in fact a denial of Christ's full humanity, arguing instead that Jesus had *two* persons, the *divine* Logos and the *human* Jesus. In his view, the human and divine persons of Christ are separate. Therefore, Nestorius preferred a title like "Mother of Christ," for Mary gave birth only to Christ's human nature.

But if Mary had not given birth to God, to whom then had she given birth? Nestorius' answer was that Mary had merely prepared a human body which was later to be assumed by the divine Christ—which reminds us of a much older heresy, Adoptionism (see 6.b). This Nestorian answer amounted to a denial of the full union of the human and divine natures of

Christ—and ultimately, a denial of his humanity, a sort of reverse of the dreaded Arian heresy, which denied Christ's divinity.

Not surprisingly, the 9th generation Church Father John Cassian describes Nestorianism as a form of Adoptionism with the following words:

> [T]hat heresy which copies and follows the lead of Pelagianism, strives and contends in every way to make it believed that the Lord Jesus Christ, the Son of God, when born of the Virgin was only a mere man; and that having afterwards taken the path of virtue He merited by His holy and pious life to be counted worthy for this holiness of His life that the Divine Majesty should unite Itself to Him: and thus by cutting off altogether from Him the honour of His sacred origin, it only left to Him the selection on account of His merits.[338]

Nestorians held that Jesus was two distinct persons, that there were two distinct persons in the Incarnate Christ, one human and the other divine—which is against the orthodox teaching that Christ was a divine person who assumed a human nature. So if in Jesus a divine person and a human person were joined in perfect harmony of action but not in the unity of a single "hypostasis," how could this harmony be explained? They could only be united by a perfect agreement of two wills in Christ, and by a harmonious communication of their respective activities. They could not be joined ontologically (in their being) or hypostatically (constituting one person), but only somehow psychologically—as if the divine person and the human person were acting "in sync."

---

[338] On the Incarnation 5:1.

The Council of Ephesus, in which the Church Father Cyril of Alexandria played a key role, condemned Nestorianism in 431, later followed by the Council of Chalcedon in 451. Both Councils clarified the orthodox Catholic view that Jesus' two natures are inseparably joined in one person. Christ is only one Person, and Mary is the mother of that Person. Mothers give birth to persons, and not natures. That's why Athanasius, the two Gregorys, and Ambrose had often used the Greek title of "Theotokos" which had been common among Christians from earliest days on. Nestorius' error was to divide Christ into two persons—human and divine. So an edict of Theodosius II in 435 ordered his writings to be burnt. Nestorius fled to Persia and gained a large, rather powerful following there. Only centuries later, the Muslims finally destroyed his sect.

c. Defenders of the Faith

Cyril of Alexandria (378-444)

Cyril succeeded Athanasius as patriarch of Alexandria, but he also succeeded him as a 9th generation Church Father defending the Catholic Faith against heresies, especially Nestorianism.

Cyril responded to Nestorius' claim that Mary was not, "strictly speaking," the Mother of God by pointing out that a mother does not give birth to a nature, but to a person:

> *[W]e call the Virgin not mother of man (ἀνθρωποτόκος) but mother of God (θεοτόκος), applying the former title to the fashioning and conception, but the latter to the union. For this cause the child who was born is called Emmanuel, neither God separated from human*

nature nor man stripped of Godhead.[339]

Since Jesus was God in the flesh, one could, "strictly speaking," talk of Mary as the Mother of God. Cyril referred to the union of deity and humanity in Jesus as the "hypostatic union":

> *For we do not say that the nature of the Word was changed and became flesh, nor that he was turned into a whole man made of body and soul. Rather do we claim that the Word in an unspeakable, inconceivable manner united to himself hypostatically flesh enlivened by a rational soul, and so became man and was called son of man, not by God's will alone or good pleasure, nor by the assumption of a person alone. Rather did two different natures come together to form a unity, and from both arose one Christ, one Son. It was not as though the distinctness of the natures was destroyed by the union, but divinity and humanity together made perfect for us one Lord and one Christ, together marvellously and mysteriously combining to form a unity. So he who existed and was begotten of the Father before all ages is also said to have been begotten according to the flesh of a woman, without the divine nature either beginning to exist in the holy virgin, or needing of itself a second begetting after that from his Father.*[340]

In the God-man Jesus, there is an indivisible unity between his divinity and humanity:

> *And the words of our Savior in the Gospels we apportion neither to two Hypostases nor Persons (for neither is the One and Only Christ two-fold, even though He be conceived to have been out of*

---

[339] Counter-statements to Cyril's 12 Anathemas 1.
[340] Letter 1.

> two diverse things gathered unto an inseverable Unity just as Man too is conceived of as of soul and body, and is not two-fold but one out of both) but thinking aright we shall maintain that both the human and besides the Divine expressions have been said by One.[341]

To make sure his explanation was not mistaken as a form of Patripassianism (see 7.b), Cyril added:

> In a similar way we say that he suffered and rose again, not that the Word of God suffered blows or piercing with nails or any other wounds in his own nature (for the divine, being without a body, is incapable of suffering), but because the body which became his own suffered these things, he is said to have suffered them for us. For he was without suffering, while his body suffered. Something similar is true of his dying. For by nature the Word of God is of itself immortal and incorruptible and life and life-giving, but since on the other hand his own body by God's grace, as the apostle says, tasted death for all, the Word is said to have suffered death for us, not as if he himself had experienced death as far as his own nature was concerned (it would be sheer lunacy to say or to think that), but because, as I have just said, his flesh tasted death.[342]

During the Synod of Alexandria, Cyril defended Mary's title of "Mother of God" and responded to Nestorius as follows:

> So God the Word was not made flesh, but assumed living and reasonable flesh. He Himself is not naturally conceived of the Virgin, fashioned, formed, and deriving beginning of existence from her; He who is before the ages,

---

[341] Third Letter to Nestorius.
[342] Letter 2.

> *God, and with God, being with the Father and with the Father both known and worshipped; but He fashioned for Himself a temple in the Virgin's womb, and was with that which was formed and begotten. Wherefore also we style that holy Virgin θεοτόκος, not because she gave birth in natural manner to God, but to man united to the God that had fashioned Him.*[343]

Following what earlier Church Fathers had confirmed before him, Cyril explained that the only-begotten Logos of God assumed flesh of the blessed Virgin, made it his own, subjected himself to human birth, and came forth from the woman as man, without casting off that which he was eternally:

> [W]e understand the form of the servant [Jesus] to have been fashioned, formed, conceived, and generated. But since the form was not stripped of the form of God, but was a Temple containing God the Word dwelling in it, according to the words of Paul For it pleased the Father that in him should all fullness dwell bodily, we call the Virgin not mother of man (ἀνθρωποτόκος) but mother of God (θεοτόκος), applying the former title to the fashioning and conception, but the latter to the union. For this cause the child who was born is called Emmanuel, neither God separated from human nature nor man stripped of Godhead.[344]

Some say Cyril's opposition to Nestorianism was the product of deep-seated rivalry and part of a power grab, but there is much to suggest that Cyril's battle with Nestorianism was the product of profound theological reflection and a lifetime of Scripture study. Cyril was much more than an ecclesiastical

---

[343] Theodoret: Counter-statements to Cyril's 12 Anathemas 1.
[344] Theodoret: Counter-statements to Cyril's 12 Anathemas 1.

politician; his thinking was shaped by the Bible, the fruit of years of patiently expounding the Scriptures verse by verse. But the conflict did come to a head when Cyril successfully petitioned the pope to declare Nestorius' views heretical. Nestorius refused to budge, however, and requested that Emperor Theodosius II call a council to settle the dispute. This request was granted, and at the Council of Ephesus Nestorius planned to denounce Cyril for heresy.

Ironically, the council's ultimate decision was exactly the opposite: it rejected Nestorianism as heretical and removed Nestorius from office. Cyril prevailed over Nestorius at the Council of Ephesus, when the bishops overwhelming acclaimed that Christ, the God-man, is a single subject, single person, single "self," in whom divine and human natures are united—and so Mary could rightly be called "Mother of God."

Cyril had made up *Twelve Anathemas* for the Council to consider, so Nestorius could respond to them. The Acts of the Council report the bishops' support for Cyril's anathemas: "All the bishops at the same time cried out: These are the sentiments (φωναί) of all of us, these are the things we all say— the accomplishment of this is the desire of us all."[345]

The Catechism of the Catholic Church summarizes this as follows:

> *The Nestorian heresy regarded Christ as a human person joined to the divine person of God's Son. Opposing this heresy, St. Cyril of Alexandria and the third ecumenical council, at*

---

[345] Council of Ephesus Acts, Decree of the Council Against Nestorius.

> *Ephesus in 431, confessed 'that the Word, uniting to himself in his person the flesh animated by a rational soul, became man.'*[346]

Faced with the heresy of Nestorius, the fourth Ecumenical Council, at Chalcedon in 451, officially declared:

> *Following the holy Fathers, we unanimously teach and confess one and the same Son, our Lord Jesus Christ: the same perfect in divinity and perfect in humanity, the same truly God and truly man, composed of rational soul and body; consubstantial with the Father as to his divinity and consubstantial with us as to his humanity; 'like us in all things but sin'. He was begotten from the Father before all ages as to his divinity and in these last days, for us and for our salvation, was born as to his humanity of the virgin Mary, the Mother of God.*[347]

It was Pope Leo the Great who put his stamp on this outcome by stressing again the Divinity of Christ:

> *He took the form of a slave without stain of sin, increasing the human and not diminishing the divine: because that emptying of Himself whereby the Invisible made Himself visible and, Creator and Lord of all things though He be, wished to be a mortal, was the bending down of pity, not the failing of power. Accordingly He who while remaining in the form of God made man, was also made man in the form of a slave. For both natures retain their own proper character without loss: and as the form of God did not do away with the form of a slave, so the*

---

[346] Catechism of the Catholic Church 466.
[347] Ibid. 467.

form of a slave did not impair the form of God.[348]

It is clear from all of this why Cyril became known as the champion of Mary's title, "the Mother of God." Thus he laid the groundwork for later developments in the Catholic Faith, such as Mary's Immaculate Conception and her Assumption into Heaven.

John Cassian (c. 360-c. 435)

Another Church Father of the 9th generation is John Cassian, probably best known as a monk and ascetic writer of Southern Gaul, and the first to introduce the rules of Eastern monasticism into the West. Benedict, the future founder of the soon to be Benedictine Order, made use of Cassian's rules in writing his own Rule, and ordered selections from his "Conferences," which he called a mirror of monasticism [*speculum monasticum*], to be read daily in his monasteries.

But Cassian did much more for the Church than introducing monasticism to the West. Another work of him, "On the Incarnation" [*De Incarnatione Domini contra Nestorium*], written at the request of the Roman Archdeacon Leo, soon to be Pope Leo the Great, was a defense of the orthodox doctrine against the errors of Nestorius. It appears to have been written hurriedly, and is, consequently, not of equal value with the other works of this author. A large part consists of proofs of Our Lord's Divinity, drawn from the Scriptures, in support of the title of Mary to be regarded as the Mother of God.

In this work, John Cassian denounces Nestorianism, which he declares as incompatible with the doctrine of the Trinity:

A most dangerous and deadly assertion indeed,

---

[348] In the Letter to Flavian, also called "The Tome," Letter 8:3.

> *which takes away what truly belongs to God, and holds out false promises to men; and which should be condemned for abominable lies on both sides, since it attacks God with wicked blasphemy, and gives to men the hope of a false assurance A most perverse and wicked assertion as it gives to men what does not belong to them, and takes away from God what is His. ... The new heresy then, as we have already many times declared, says that the Lord Jesus Christ was born of the Virgin Mary, only a mere man: and so that Mary should be called* Christotocos *not* Theotocos, *because she was the mother of Christ, not of God.*[349]

Denying that Mary is the Mother of God also puts her virginity into question. Mary's virginity had already been attacked earlier, notably by Helvidius, who argued that Jesus could only be called the first-born if others were born to the same mother. However, his arguments had already been discredited by Jerome:

> *Our position is this: Every only begotten son is a first-born son, but not every first-born is an only begotten. By first-born we understand not only one who is succeeded by others, but one who has had no predecessor. Everything, says the Lord to Aaron, that opens the womb of all flesh which they offer unto the Lord, both of man and beast, shall be yours: nevertheless the first born of man shall you surely redeem, and the firstling of unclean beasts shall you redeem. The word of God defines first-born as everything that opens the womb. Otherwise, if the title belongs to such only as have younger brothers, the priests cannot claim the firstlings until their successors have been begotten, lest, perchance, in case there were*

---

[349] On the Incarnation 5:1.

> *no subsequent delivery it should prove to be the first-born but not merely the only begotten.*[350]

Cassian asks a rather simple question: if Jesus was a mere man, why had his birth to be prepared so miraculously? Apparently, his birth was not merely a matter of what he called "flesh-from-flesh":

> *If only a mere man was to be born of a pure virgin why should there be such careful mention of the Divine Advent? Why such intervention of Divinity itself? Certainly if only a man was to be born from man, and flesh from flesh, a command alone might have done it, or the Divine will. ... And so the Word, the Son, descended: the majesty of the Holy Ghost was present: the power of the Father was overshadowing; that in the mystery of the holy conception the whole Trinity might cooperate.*[351]

Nestorians like to say that mothers cannot give birth to what precedes them in time, and that it is impossible for God to be born of a woman. Cassian considers those arguments "foolish" because it is not the God in Jesus that is born of a woman, but the man in Jesus:

> *And so you say, O heretic, whoever you may be, who deny that God was born of the Virgin, that Mary the Mother of our Lord Jesus Christ ought not to be called* Theotocos, *i.e., Mother of God, but* Christotocos, *i.e., only the Mother of Christ, not of God. For no one, you say, brings forth what is anterior in time. And of this utterly foolish argument whereby you think that the birth of God can be understood by carnal minds, and fancy that the mystery of His Majesty can be*

---

[350] Perpetual Virginity of Blessed Mary 12.
[351] On the Incarnation 2:1.

> *accounted for by human reasoning, we will, if God permits, say something later on. In the meanwhile we will now prove by Divine testimonies that Christ is God, and that Mary is the Mother of God.*[352]

Cassian's reasoning is ultimately based on a simple syllogism: if Jesus is God, and Mary is the mother of Jesus, then Mary is the Mother of God (QED):

> *Therefore the Lord Jesus Christ is God. But if He be, as He certainly is, God: then she who bore God is Theotocos, i.e., the mother of God. Unless perhaps you want to take refuge in so utterly absurd and blasphemous a contradiction as to deny that she from whom God was born is the mother of God, while you cannot deny that He who was born is God.*[353]

Cassian wants to make clear that Jesus could not be the Son of man unless he had first been the Son of God:

> *To begin with then I ask you this: Do you say that our Lord Jesus Christ, who was born of the Virgin Mary is only the Son of man, or that He is the Son of God as well? For we, I mean all who hold the Catholic faith, all of us, I say, believe and are sure and know and confess that He is both, i.e., that He is Son of man because born of a woman and Son of God because conceived of Divinity. Do you then admit that He is both, i.e., Son of God and Son of man, or do you say that He is Son of man only? If Son of man only then there cry out against you apostles and prophets, aye and the Holy Ghost Himself, by whom the conception was brought about. ... Do you see how Jesus Christ is first proclaimed to be the Son of*

---

[352] Ibid. 2:2.
[353] Ibid. 2:5.

> *God that according to the flesh He might become the Son of man? For when the Virgin Mary was to bring forth the Lord she conceived owing to the descent of the Holy Spirit upon her and the cooperation of the power of the Most High. ... He could not be the Son of man unless He had first been the Son of God.*[354]

We have here the Mystery of the eternal God dwelling in the lowliness of Jesus' body:

> *He was the same Person then on earth who was also in heaven: the same Person in His low estate who was also in the highest: the same Person in the littleness of manhood as in the glory of the Godhead. ... At the very time of His conception as man there came all the power of God, all the fullness of the Godhead; for thence came all the perfection of the Godhead, whence was His origin. Nor was that Human nature of His ever without the Deity as it received from Deity the very fact of its existence. ... [R]emember that whatever you read of Christ you read of the Son of God: whatever you read of the Lord or Jesus belongs to the Son of God.*[355]

Yet, we can never separate what we find always united in the God-man Jesus, in him who is the Son of God and the Son of man at the same time. In other words, Jesus is at the same time the Son of Man, born on Earth, and the Son of God, abiding in Heaven:

> *Consider then this at last, and note that the Son of man is the same Person as the Word of God: for He is the Son of man since He is truly born of man, and the Word of God, since He who speaks*

---

[354] Ibid. 2:6.
[355] Ibid. 2:7.

> *on earth abides ever in heaven. And so when He truly terms Himself the Son of man, it refers to His human birth, while the fact that He never departs from heaven, refers to the Infinite character of His Divine nature.*[356]

Therefore, there is no division in Jesus that would make him two Persons. There is in Christ only one and a single Personal self:

> *Because the apostles took every possible precaution that it might not be thought that there was any division in Christ, or that the Son of God being joined to a Son of man, might come by wild interpretations to be made into two Persons, and thus He who is in Himself but one might by wrongful and wicked notions of ours, be made into a double Person in one nature.*[357]

Did Cassian finally and effectively end the controversy? Probably not. Heresies lead multiple lives and keep popping up in various disguises. And there are still Christians nowadays who stick with certain heresies—knowingly or unknowingly. But at least we have an impressive series of Church Fathers here to keep us on the right track. They go on proclaiming the truth as to what Jesus has told us. As long as their voices are being heard, Jesus will be heard.

Cassian closes our series of Church Fathers in this book. Were there more Church Fathers after Cassian? Yes, there were. Names that come to mind are Benedict of Nursia, Caesarius of Arles, Fulgentius of Ruspe, Gregory of Tours, Severus of Antioch, and last but not least John of Damascus. However, I decided to limit our discussion to those Church Fathers who defended us against the most devastating

---

[356] Ibid. 4:6.
[357] Ibid. 5:7.

heresies, which would have corrupted the Catholic Faith to the core had they taken hold of the Catholic Faith. For that reason, I thought, they would deserve special attention in this book. They helped us keeping the Faith in times of trouble.

11. Conclusion

Many of us might still feel like Emperor Constantine—wondering what the fuss is all about. The Nicene Creed may appear to us like a case of theological hairsplitting, yet it was an issue Christians were willing to die for. What may also disturb some is how a single iota in the middle of a single Greek word would be able to create so much rioting, fighting, killing, and exiling. However, the truth may very well be in the details. The Creed is the "Faith of our Fathers" for which Christian citizens of the Roman Empire suffered imprisonment and death. G. K. Chesterton once said, "Truths turn into dogmas the instant that they are disputed."[358] And the late, great Dorothy Sayers would add to this that the drama is in the dogma, for which our ancestors were willing to die:

> *Official Christianity, of late years, has been having what is known as bad press. We are constantly assured that the churches are empty because preachers insist too much upon doctrine—dull dogma as people call it. The fact is the precise opposite. It is the neglect of dogma that makes for dullness. The Christian faith is the most exciting drama that ever staggered the imagination of man—and the dogma is the drama.*[359]

---

[358] Heretics (New York: John Lane Company, 1905), 304.
[359] *Letters to a Diminished Church: Passionate Arguments for*

The Church Fathers are, in the minds of many, associated with dogmas. Unfortunately, dogmas are not very popular nowadays. Even the new General of the Jesuits recently said, "Doctrine is a word that I don't like very much, it brings with it the image of the hardness of stone. Instead, the human reality is much more nuanced, it is never black or white, it is in continual development." Ironically, it's precisely because human reality is not black and white that we need the rock-hard reality of dogma. Dogmas give us certainty in the midst of the many uncertainties of life; they console us with certainties that we'd never have without God's revelation. One of these is the dogma of the Incarnation: God became human flesh for our salvation—the certainty that there is hope for us after death. That's also the reason why dogmas never change: they are rocks of certainty under the sometimes turbulent waves of daily life.

This was very well expressed by the Catholic writer Flannery O'Connor. She calls dogmas "windows to the infinite" and "guardians of mystery."[360] Therefore she could say as an author, "I write with a solid belief in all the Christian dogmas." Dogmas don't give her the feel of restriction but of freedom: "For me a dogma is only a gateway to contemplation and is an instrument of freedom and not of restriction."[361] We should be grateful to the Church Fathers for opening for us this gateway to contemplation.

We found out in this book that the "First Christians"—whom we could easily call the "First Catholics" (see 1.c)—are not much different from Catholics nowadays, at least not in their beliefs. They may not use the exact same words and

---

the Relevance of Christian Doctrine. Thomas Nelson, 2004.

[360] *The Habit of Being: Letters of Flannery O'Connor*, (New York: The Noonday Press/Farrar, Straus and Giroux, 1979).

[361] *The Habit of Being: Letters of Flannery O'Connor*, p. 92.

The First Christians: Keeping the Faith in Times of Trouble

wordings as Catholics do today, but their beliefs are basically the same, in spite of having gone through a stream of twenty centuries. We all go back to the "Word made Flesh," to the Jesus that the apostles and their successors have handed down to us.

Those who think differently and believe that the Catholic Church veered off and polluted the original Faith of the Early Christians, should at least think twice. After reading the Church Fathers, perhaps the biggest discovery is that the first Christians were actually Catholics like we are. Thanks to the Fathers of the Early Church, the Catholic Church was able to navigate around the many road-blocks of heresy. Owing to the Church Fathers, the Church was able to stay on track—the track that Jesus had outlined for her. Cardinal John Newman, a Catholic convert from Anglicanism, once wrote, "The principles and proceedings of the Church now, were those of the Church then; the principles and proceedings of heretics then, were those of Protestants now."[362] And Steve Ray, a Catholic convert coming from the Evangelical church, would discover after his conversion that the Protestant Reformation was not a recovery of what had been lost, but rather a radical departure from what had always been.

Nevertheless, some Christians—in the sense of Christians who distinguish themselves from Catholics—still think that the Catholic Church was the result of the "Great Apostasy" mentioned in 2 Thess. 2:3. So they claim that the date of founding of the Catholic Church was not in the 1st century, but in the 4th century when Emperor Constantine made it the official religion of the Roman Empire. After Catholicism

---

[362] *Apologia pro Vita Sua*, edited by Ian Ker, London, Penguin Books, 1994, p. 114.

became the accepted religion of the Roman Empire in 312, the Catholic Church was infiltrated by paganism, they say. Pagan Roman priests rushed to get new jobs as priests in the new official religion of *Roman* Catholicism. So the actual founder of Catholicism is allegedly not Jesus but the Roman Emperor Constantine. Thus took place what Mormons and Jehovah's Witnesses much later called the "Great Apostasy"—an enormous collapse of the Truth.

However, instead of a "Great Apostasy," we have a "Great Myth" here, created by enemies of the Catholic Church. Nicaea was not imposed by the Roman Empire or Emperor Constantine, as we discovered earlier (see 8.b). What connects Nicaea with Jesus Christ is an impressive chain of Church Fathers who painstakingly followed Christ and defended his message in an uncorrupted manner. And Constantine is not the beginning of corruption in the Church. Everything that happened before or after Constantine is kept in line by the Church Fathers, who faithfully held on to what Jesus had taught us through the apostles. The Fathers are our testimony *against* the "puritanical" and anti-Catholic belief that the original and initial Christian Church has been covered over with creeds and doctrines of mere men.

But also those who swear by the doctrine of "Scripture Only" miss out on the vital role the Church Fathers have played in the protection of what Jesus has told us. Many Protestants still look at the history of Christianity as if nothing happened between the year 100 and the year 1517 when Martin Luther promulgated his theses. However, we cannot just ignore the vital role the Church Fathers played handing down to us what Jesus had taught us. When looking for witnesses, we want people who were closest to the action, for they have usually a better perspective than those who are far removed. They are in a direct line of generations with the apostles, and thus with Jesus himself. It is not *their* message but *his* message that they proclaim. So also, it is not *our* message but *his* message that we believe in, so we want to learn from the Church Fathers what Jesus' message was so that his message becomes our message.

It is always a timeless temptation to start a "cult of personality," by saying "We are of Basil," or "We are of Arius." No, "We are neither—we are of Christ." When Jesus is not mentioned, something is seriously wrong. The Apostle Paul had to fight this temptation already during the first generation of Christians:

> *For it has been reported to me about you, my brothers, by Chloe's people, that there are rivalries among you. I mean that each of you is saying, "I belong to Paul," or "I belong to Apollos," or "I belong to Cephas," or "I belong to Christ." Is Christ divided? Was Paul crucified for you? Or were you baptized in the name of Paul?*[363]

Even during times of serious persecution, Church Father Dionysius of Alexandria (200-265), also known as "the Great," dared to compare those who save unity in the Church with those who lose their lives during persecutions: "a martyrdom borne for the sake of preventing a division of the Church, would not have been more inglorious than one endured for refusing to worship idols; nay, in my opinion at least, the former would have been a nobler thing than the latter."[364] As a matter of fact, the narcissist, through his own perverted "cult of personality," obstructs the view of Christ. Christianity is all about Jesus, whether for the first generation or the latest generation of Christians. That is the

---

[363] 1 Cor. 1:11-13.
[364] Epistle 2: to Novatus.

lasting message the Church Fathers have for us. All we can hope and pray that their message keeps resounding.

12. For Further Reading

For translations of the writings of the Fathers, we used the so-called "thirty-eight volume set," published between 1867 and 1900. These texts can also be found on the *New Advent* website: http://www.newadvent.org/fathers/ (Copyright © 2009 by Kevin Knight). Their translation is not always smooth and user-friendly, but it is easy to look up the passages we quoted in this book, so the reader can see them in their context.

For Bible quotations, we used the *New American Bible*, which can also be easily accessed on the Internet through the website of the United States Conference of Bishops: http://usccb.org/bible/books-of-the-bible/index.cfm.

Akin, Jimmy. *The Fathers Know Best – Your Essential Guide to the Teaching*. San Diego, CA: Catholic Answers Press, 2010.

Aquilina, Mike. *The Fathers of the Church – An Introduction to the First Christian Teachers*. Huntington, IN: Our Sunday Visitor Publishing Division, 1999.

Benedict XVI. *Jesus, the Apostles and the Early Church*. San Francisco, CA: Ignatius Press, 2007.

Bennett, Rod. *Four Witnesses – The Early Church in her Own Words*. San Francisco, CA: Ignatius Press, 2002.

Bennett, Rod. *The Apostasy That Wasn't – The Extraordinary Story of the Unbreakable Early Church*. San Diego, CA: Catholic Answers Press, 2015.

D'Ambrosio, Marcellino. *When the Church Was Young – Voice of the Early Fathers*. Cincinnati, OH: Servant Books, 2014.

Kreeft, Peter. *Catholic Christianity: A Complete Catechism of Catholic Beliefs based on the Catechism of the Catholic Church*. San Francisco, CA: Ignatius Press, 2001.

Sayers, Dorothy. *The Emperor Constantine*. Grand Rapids, MI: Eerdmans Publishing, 1976),

Stark, Rodney. *The Rise of Christianity*. San Francisco, CA: Harper, 1997.

13. Index

A

Adoptionism 128-29, 132-33, 135, 158, 166, 235-36

Alexander of Alexandria 156, 165, 167, 180

Alexandria...50, 106, 111, 125, 130, 167, 181

Ambrose..... 205, 209, 237

anathema 8, 241

Antoninus 71, 90

apologist 71, 87, 88

Apostolic Fathers.... 51, 84

apostolic succession 59-60, 65-6, 83, 100-101, 161, 175, 180

Arianism........157, 164-68, 170, 172-75, 178, 181, 183, 186, 189, 191, 195-96, 206-09, 233

Arius....17, 165-69, 171-72, 176, 180, 207, 255

Athanasius of Alexandria 5, 171, 175, 180

Augustine117, 142, 143, 209, 211, 218-29

Augustine of Canterbury 233

Augustus 19-20

B

baptism29, 44, 53, 128, 132, 141-42, 160, 194, 212, 220, 224

Basil of Caesarea .. 181-82, 186

Bede 215

Belloc, Hilaire..............173

Benedict XVI 18, 33, 78

Bennett, Rod.....11, 32, 211

Beryllus.......................132

Bible.....3-6, 29, 31, 47, 56, 61, 214-16, 219, 241

Bible, canon....4-6, 31, 181

C

Calvin, John 11, 223

Cardinal George 26

Cassian 236, 243, 245-46, 248

catacombs 75

Chesterton, G. K. .. 146, 251

Clement of Alexandria 106, 111, 115, 117, 119

Clement of Rome 51, 56, 63, 66, 84, 124

Coliseum 72

Constantine 163, 169, 171, 180-81, 186, 206-08, 213, 251, 253-54

Constantius 163, 208

Constantius II 195-96

Council in Jerusalem 37

Council of Constantinople 186, 191, 194, 214

Council of Ephesus 213, 237, 241

Council of Nicaea .. 175-76, 180, 191, 206-07

Cyprian5, 125-26, 129, 135-43, 221

Cyril of Alexandria 237, 241

D

Damasus I 6, 214

Decius 125-26, 129-30, 136

Didache 5, 44-7

Diocletian 145-47, 150-51, 210

Dionysius of Alexandria 255

Docetism 53-5, 62-3, 65, 67-9, 76-8, 82, 94, 98, 166

dogma 185, 251-52

Domitian 49

Donatism 110, 130, 209-11, 216-17, 219-21, 226, 233

Douay-Rheims Bible ... 215

E

Ebionism 27-9, 31, 34, 36-7, 41-2, 46, 54, 67, 69,

76-8, 98

ecclesia 21

Edict of Milan 164, 213

Epistle to Diognetus 51

Eucharist 21, 44, 46, 61, 66-7, 69, 91, 185

Eusebius 20, 34, 44, 56, 62, 82-3, 109, 126-27, 130, 132, 180

F

free will 211, 221, 223-5

G

Gallerius 145, 206

Gallienus 145

generation 2, 7-8, 10-11, 18

Gnosticism 54, 76-80, 90, 94, 108, 111

Gregory of Nazianzus . 181, 186, 209

Gregory of Nyssa. 182, 191, 214

Gregory the Great 231, 233-4

H

Helvidius 244

heresy 8

Hilary 195-204, 209

Holy Spirit 4, 37-8, 63, 79, 90, 97, 108-10, 116, 120, 124, 128, 131-32, 135, 149-50, 182-85, 187-88, 191-94, 226-29, 247

homoousios ... 170-72, 198, 208

human freedom 221-23, 225

hypostatic union 238

I

Ignatius of Antioch. 13, 34, 47, 51, 63, 75, 80, 84

Irenaeus 8, 56, 79-80, 82, 84, 90, 93-103, 124

Islam 173-75

J

Jerome 208, 213-220, 244

John of Damascus 174, 248

John Paul II 70

Julian the Apostate ... 164, 176, 214

Julius Caesar 19-20

Justin30, 72, 74, 85-93, 111, 114, 119

K

King James Version 47, 215

L

Lactantius146, 148, 150-56

lapsi 126, 129

Leo the Great . 231, 242-43

Lewis, C. S. 166, 176

Lubac, Henri de 234

Luther, Martin 215, 223, 254

M

Marcion ... 31, 77, 83-4, 119

Marcus Aurelius .. 71-2, 88, 93

Messiah 22-4, 36, 53

Modalism120, 129, 148-52, 157-58, 160, 167, 182, 208

Monarchianism 129

Montanism 108-10, 115, 117, 120, 122, 129

Montanus 17, 108-09

Mother of God235, 237-46

Muratorian Canon 5

N

Nazarenes 30

Nero.19-20, 25, 34, 49, 71, 93

Nestorianism. 235-37, 240-41, 243

Nestorius 235-43

Newman, John 253

Nicene Creed15, 175, 181, 194, 208-09, 251

Novatian 126, 129, 137, 139, 156

Novatianism128, 136-37, 139, 210

O

O'Connor, Flannery....211, 252

Origen...5, 29, 56, 111, 118, 125, 130-4

original sin......211-12, 217, 223

Original Sin................223

P

Patripassianism....148-49, 154-55, 159-60, 239

Paul..................9

Pelagianism 209, 211, 213, 216-19, 221-22, 226, 232, 236

Peter..24, 25, 32-8, 40-1, 51, 56, 62-3, 65, 79, 89-90, 96, 99-100, 123, 158, 164, 216, 231-32

Pius IX.................22

Pliny..................49

Polycarp 13, 51, 64, 75, 80-5, 93, 101, 106

Praxeas. 120, 122, 128, 148

presbyter 38, 47, 57-62, 66, 83, 102, 127

priest............47, 60-2, 66

proselyte................28

R

Ray, Stephen............12

ressourcement............7

Revelation...........33, 85

Roman Catholic. 13-5, 254

S

Sabbath. 29-30, 36, 46, 69

Sabellianism........148, 158

Sabellius 148, 158, 171, 199

sacraments. 210, 217, 220-1, 225

Saltzman, Russell.........78

Sayers, Dorothy.. 180, 251

schism 8-11, 14, 28-9, 38, 58, 110, 126, 134-39, 143, 219, 221, 235

Septimius Severus......105

Septuagint...........28, 214

Simon Peter .....(see Peter)

Simon the Magician 89

Sozomen 186

Stark, Rodney . 50, 52, 138

Stephen 39-40

Suetonius 24

T

Tacitus 20, 25

Tertullian...56, 71, 105-07, 111, 117-24, 128, 182

Theodore...... 171, 175, 206

Theodoret....164, 169, 175, 206

Theodosius.......186-7, 191, 206, 209, 232

Theodosius II...... 237, 241

Tiberius........19-20, 25, 93

Tradition...6, 18, 100, 103, 117, 134, 190, 227

Trajan............................49

Trinity 120-3, 132, 135, 149, 173, 175, 182-83, 186-96, 208, 226-7, 243, 245

Tyler Hitchcock, Susan 50

V

Valentianism 94, 98

Valerian 126, 136, 142

Vatican II 142-43

Vincent of Lérins 16-17

Vulgate...................214-15

About the Author

Gerard M. Verschuuren is a human geneticist who also earned a doctorate in the philosophy of science. He studied and worked at universities in Europe and the United States. Currently semi-retired, he spends most of his time as a writer, speaker, and consultant on the interface of science and religion, faith and reason.

Some of his most recent books are:

- The Destiny of the Universe—In Pursuit of the Great Unknown. (St. Paul, MN: Paragon House, 2014).
- Five Anti-Catholic Myths—Slavery, Crusades, Inquisition, Galileo, and Holocaust. (Kettering, OH: Angelico Press, 2015).
- Aquinas and Modern Science—A Match Made in Heaven. (Kettering, OH: Angelico Press, 2016).
- The Myth of an Anti-Science Church—Galileo, Darwin, Teilhard, Hawking, Dawkins. (Upcoming).
- Religion under Siege: The Eclipse of God. (St. Louis, MO: En Route Books and Media, 2018).
- Faith and Reason: The Cradle of Truth. (St. Louis, MO: En Route Books and Media, 2017).
- Anti-Catholic Fabrications—Forty Myths Exposed.

For more information, see the following Wikipedia page:

http://en.wikipedia.org/wiki/Gerard_Verschuuren

Dr. Verschuuren may be contacted at www.where-do-we-come-from.com

www.ingramcontent.com/pod-product-compliance
Lightning Source LLC
Chambersburg PA
CBHW032151080426
42735CB00008B/665